Methods of
Spiritual Research

by

Rudolf Steiner

D1464765

MULTIMEDIA PUBLISHING CORP.
Blauvelt, New York 10913, U.S.A.
1973

The authorized translation for the Western Hemisphere by agreement with the Rudolf Steiner-Nachlassverwaltung, Dornach-bei-Basel, Switzerland.

Library of Congress Catalog Card Number 75-150427

Manufactured in the United States of America

Contents

Man as a Being of Spirit and Soul

The science of spirit, about which I have had the honor to lecture for many years now, here in Stuttgart, as well as in other places, is, I believe, based upon a need arising out of the cultural and spiritual life of the present time. It does not arise simply because someone may feel it to be a good idea. In order to realize that it is just at the present time that this science has to make a start, it is perhaps necessary to see how particular spiritual impulses arise at certain moments during the whole evolution of human spiritual and cultural life. It is not so difficult to see that the science of spirit has a connection with the present time similar to the connection that the Copernican outlook had with its time. Just as the latter could not have existed at an earlier period, so, too, with the science of spirit. We only have to compare, on the basis of true knowledge, the way the scientific outlook obtains its results — and has obtained them for some time — with the way this outlook is taken up by the widest circles of humanity in order to provide a basis for questions concerning the soul and the spirit. We need only to look at the method of research and the way it has spread and to compare it with the scientific outlook of centuries ago, which had prevailed for thousands of years of human evolution. In those earlier times people looked at nature and its phenomena in quite a different way from today and the last two, three, four hundred years. In earlier times when people looked at nature and its processes they took something spiritual, something of a soul nature, into their own soul and spirit life. It was not like today when the phenomena of nature are investigated purely as phenomena, as far as possible eliminating everything of a spirit-soul nature.

This is not a criticism of the modern scientific outlook — on the contrary. The success of the scientific outlook, which certainly has a significant purpose both for the present and the future, is due to its efforts to eliminate everything of a spirit-soul nature from the observation of natural phenomena. It concentrates solely on observing processes in nature without bringing into these processes anything of a spirit-soul nature. On the other hand it has become absolutely necessary to satisfy the unquenchable need of the human soul to approach the great riddles of existence scientifically from a different viewpoint. It is just because natural science has to keep to its serious and conscientious method and is obliged to eliminate spirit-soul nature that a science of spirit, based on the example and ideal of natural science, must take its place alongside natural science, working in the same way as natural science, but from different sources.

It cannot be said that the present time has got very far in formulating a view about the relationship of natural science to any endeavors of a more spiritually scientific kind. It is just the most serious questions about the life of the soul and the spirit, about the eternal nature of the being of man, about human freedom and all that is connected with it, that are excluded and have been banned from the outlook based on natural science since the middle of the 19th century. And it is a fact that great and outstanding scientists of the present time find themselves in a strange position. We have already seen how it is only recently that outstanding scientists have shaken off the scientific romanticism of Darwinism prevalent in the second half of the 19th century.

We could take hundreds of scientists and thinkers to illustrate our point, but we shall take one as an example. We have seen how a scientist like Oskar Hertwig has managed to bring the fantastic tendencies of naturalism, which have threatened to run wild, back on to a saner basis. And a book such as Oskar Hertwig's *Das Werden der Organismen, Eine Darwinische Zufallstheorie*, a book by an eminent pupil of Haeckel, — such a book, even from a scientific viewpoint, has great significance. Much could be added in this respect that is equally significant or nearly so. We can see from such achievements, which cannot be sufficiently recognized in their own sphere, what predicament serious scientists are in regarding questions of the soul and spirit. In reading Oskar Hertwig's influential book we have just referred to, we cannot help being aware of a certain feeling or attitude toward questions of spiritual life. We find that a scientist like Oskar Hertwig makes quite clear that he cannot approach questions of the soul or spirit with the means at his disposal, the means of a stringent science. On one page he says this clearly and definitely: Science can only concern itself with the transitory sense world; science cannot approach the eternal in human nature.

So far, so good — and one would think that the way is now open for a science of spirit, for the scientist himself points out that a science of spirit should exist alongside natural science. But, unfortunately, there is something else to be found among scientists, which is not said explicitly, but which can be read quite clearly between the lines. The opinion is spread abroad — albeit unconsciously — that the method employed by the scientist is the only exact one, and that it is possible to be scientific only so long as one keeps to the outer sense world. — People then believe that a departure from the sense world is bound to lead into a world of fantasy and dreams. — What is so dangerous in this is that it is not clearly expressed, but arises as a kind of feeling out of what is achieved and spreads into the widest circles of people. It is to be found in those who believe they understand a lot about the scientific outlook and wish to draw conclusions affecting spiritual life from the scientific outlook, and also in those who think themselves enlightened because they read the supplement of their local paper every Sunday which breathes this kind of feeling I have described as spreading into the widest circles.

Thus, on the one hand, the scientific outlook points with great emphasis to the need for the coming into being of a science of spirit, but on the other it takes the ground away from under its feet. This was crystallized in a famous speech by Dubois-Reymond, the great physiologist, which I have referred to here in Stuttgart, and which he gave before an obviously enlightened meeting of scientists in Leipzig in the 70's. It was crystallized in his lecture, *The Limits of Natural Knowledge,* where he stated that natural knowledge is not able to give any information about even the simplest phenomena of the life of the soul, and that science comes to an end where the supersensible begins. — With this it is admitted on the one hand that natural science is not able to say anything about the supersensible, but on the other it emphatically takes away the ground for all supersensible investigation. The science of spirit has to struggle against these aims and efforts today. For it sets out to face and treat scientifically the questions which the human soul turns to in great longing — the question of the eternal nature of the human soul, of the freedom of human action and the countless other questions which are connected to these two main questions.

But now from another viewpoint we come to much the same result. If in trying to inform ourselves about such matters we turn, not to science, but to the work of philosophers, we find just as little satisfaction there. What is offered is, on the whole, — for someone really seeking spiritual substance in cultural life — nothing more than a collection of abstract concepts, which do not offer anything pertaining to the pressing questions about the life of the human soul and spirit. But it is perhaps just in this subject that we can ascertain why it is not possible at the present time to find out anything substantial about these questions outside the actual sphere of the science of spirit. And it is just the work of philosophers which reveals something rather odd, which is also the reason why I have called today's lecture a study of man as a being of spirit and soul.

In looking into a modern textbook on psychology or into

anything philosophical in order to inform ourselves about the questions we are considering, we come across a way of regarding things which, even if we go beyond purely materialistic thinking, is completely tied up with the idea that man is a being of body and soul. This idea of man as a being of body and soul governs the enlightened and impressive philosophers of today. It is therefore imperative to show that this outlook leads us astray when it comes to investigating the complete being of man. If in investigating the human being we start with the premise that everything that arises in connection with the soul and body should be divided into body and soul, we are doing the same as a chemist who assumes from the start that a substance he is investigating can have only two constituent parts. Therefore when he makes his chemical analysis, he finds he cannot get very far. Another person discovers that a result was not possible because the substance the chemist took was composed of three elements, and not of two as the chemist had imagined. It is just the same with the way people look at the being of man. It is imagined that we have to find two elements, body and soul. In fact, we can make progress only by dividing the being of man into three parts: body, soul and spirit. Otherwise, we always arrive at an impossible mix-up between spirit and soul, which is no more use for acquiring enlightenment concerning the human being than a mix-up of the bodily life and soul life which comes about through not differentiating them properly. What is really meant by dividing man not only into a being with a soul and a body on the one hand, but into a being with a soul and a spirit on the other, becomes clear in looking at the way the physical sciences of man, biology, physiology, anatomy, and so on, arise out of purely human experience, out of the experience of physical life of the human being. Let us take a particular case. The human being experiences hunger, satisfaction, need to breathe, and so on, in life. These are immediate, I would like to say, inner experiences. In the first place they are really dependent on material substances, but hunger, satisfaction, the need to breathe, are also experienced in the soul. The scientist investigates the bodily basis of hunger, satisfaction, the need to breathe, and the like. If we want to found a physical science, a science of the human body, we cannot stop at the fact that hunger is experienced in different ways. If we wanted to experience being very hungry or not very hungry, very thirsty or not very thirsty, or different kinds of hunger or thirst, we would not be able to found a science of the physical body. We have to go beyond the purely inner experience and investigate the body with scientific methods. We then discover that hunger, thirst, the need to breathe, evolve certain chemical, physical processes in the physical body and we arrive at a physiological and biological science of man. We have to go beyond what we experience purely inwardly, and subject the body by itself to scientific investigation.

Just as on the one hand we have to go beyond our immediate experience to lay the basis for a physical science, just as the body provides the physical basis for our soul experience, so on the other we have to go beyond our soul experience to find the spiritual reality that underlies it.

In examining our physical nature the ordinary scientist discovers certain physical processes in the digestive system which correspond to the inner experiences of hunger, thirst and the need to breathe. The question is bound to arise: Is there something — if I may use what is naturally a paradoxical expression — that corresponds to the soul experience from the other direction, which could be called a kind of "spiritual digestion" as compared to physical digestion? Of course it sounds like a paradox, speaking on the one hand about ordinary digestion, which is perfectly acceptable because it belongs to the province of a recognized science, and on the other hand about a spiritual digestion, a change which takes place in the spirit. Nevertheless we shall attempt to show today that this paradoxical expression does in fact correspond to a real situation.

It is no more possible to arrive at a science of spirit by investigating inwardly the nature of the soul, which surges to and fro in our thinking, feeling and willing as our inner experience, than it is to found a physical science only on the basis of an inward observation of hunger, thirst, and the need for breath. We have to appreciate that as far as our normal, everyday consciousness is concerned, our physical nature only reveals its outer surface. What does the human being in his everyday life know about all the complicated processes, the physical, chemical processes, which physical science brings to the light of day as the basis of what we experience as hunger, thirst and the need to breathe? Just compare what we see of the body in everyday life, which is more or less its outward form, its capacity for movement, its physiognomy, just compare this, which is something everyone can know about without bothering about science, with the picture of the human being as shown in anatomy, physiology or biology, and you will see how our ordinary experience of our bodies is related to the investigation of science.

But now on the other hand it is also a fact that the spirit reveals itself no more to the human being than does the body reveal itself beyond its outward form, and that from the sphere of the spirit just as little or just as much is hidden to the human being as is hidden to him in ordinary life of those processes which have first to be investigated by science.

What is it then that belongs to the spirit which is actually orientated toward our inner experience? We shall see today that the part of his spiritual life that is orientated toward the human being, but which he does not always even recognize as such, is nothing other than what is encompassed in the simple, unequivocal but significant word "I." This "I" we shall see belongs to the spirit, but it is related to the whole spirit in the same way that our outward form, our physiognomy, the movement of our limbs which is all orientated toward the ordinary body, are related to physiology, biology, to the science of the body. We can never arrive at a science of the body by feeling a little or very hungry, or by comparing one state of hunger with another, or by immersing ourselves in our hunger; neither can we arrive at a science of the spirit of the human being by immersing ourselves in our experience of feeling, thinking and imagination. We have to realize that so-called mysticism, which is supposed to be an immersion in one's own inner being, and which seeks to experience this inner being in a somewhat different way from our normal experience, that mysticism, this kind of inward immersion, cannot lead to a science of spirit any more than a differentiated experience of hunger, thirst and the need to breathe can lead to a science of the body. We have to start with our purely inner experience of hunger and thirst and proceed from there to the body, to the things that are arrived at through scientific method. Likewise we have to start with our purely mystical soul life and proceed from there to what lies spiritually outside this soul life. And this spiritual nature has naturally to be investigated according to scientific method in the strictest possible way, just as the life of the human body is investigated.

Now it is true that the methods of investigating spiritual life are in fact spiritual, and therefore are quite different from the means employed by natural science. And so my first task is to indicate the purpose and significance of the methods used by the science of spirit. It is not possible to embark upon the investigation of spiritual life without first having arrived at certain things in ordinary, everyday soul life. Without having reached a certain point in our ordinary soul life, in which we follow the course of our own inner being, we are not able to train ourselves to be a scientist of spirit. As long as we are satisfied with our ordinary, everyday soul life, as long as we derive full satisfaction from mystical experience and revel in it in order to immerse ourselves in our soul life, we shall never be able to train ourselves as real scientists of spirit. The preliminary qualification for the science of spirit is that in a particular respect we feel the insufficiency of our ordinary soul life as a result of our own experience of it.

I have pointed out in earlier lectures that it is particularly a study of the so-called border areas of science that can help us to acquire this feeling. In dealing with this subject I am fond of citing a really significant question which arises in connection with these border areas, and which the eminent scientist, Friedrich Theodor Vischer, came upon as he was struggling to clarify his own outlook. He came to ask — and you can find this in his beautiful treatise, *Die Traumphantasie* — what is the real connection between the soul and the bodily nature? And here he lighted upon a real question relating to the border-area of human knowledge. Vischer says: it is quite certain that the soul nature cannot be in the bodily nature, but it is also just as certain that it cannot be sought outside the body. — Hence he arrives at a complete contradiction. Such contradictions often arise where we do not simply consider knowledge as concerning outward, tangible facts alone, but where we really have to struggle inwardly to acquire our knowledge. Those who know what it is to have to struggle for knowledge speak of hundreds of such border-points occurring in knowledge. It is only a superficial mind which, when faced with such questions, is content to say that human cognition can go only a certain distance and no further. In contenting ourselves with this information, we are blocking our own way to a real science of spirit. For here we are not concerned with evolving all sorts of logical thoughts about such questions, but with steeping our wrestling souls in them and really experiencing them, and this means giving up the logical approach where it can no longer be applied. We have to get to the heart of what for normal human cognition is a contradiction in such a border-area, and feel the full weight of it on our souls.

If we do not simply regard these questions as comfortable cushions upon which to rest and proceed no further, but if on the contrary we really seek to experience them, then we find that it is just what lives and moves in such a living contradiction that kindles our inner soul life in a way that does not happen in normal life, that it is at just such a point as this that our inner soul life can reach a stage beyond its normal experience. In order not to become lost when we reach such a point in the experience of a border-area, we have to be able to grasp inwardly how in certain moments of his life the human being is unable to get beyond himself, but yet is able to point to something beyond himself. What is needed is that a particular inner feeling is developed which can be the result of living at such border-points of knowledge. This feeling can be characterized in the following words. It can be characterized very easily, for the experience which this feeling brings is something that cuts deep down into the soul. If we experience the questions of the border-areas properly, we do not say that there are limits to human knowledge, but we say that we are unable to cross the threshold with all the things we have acquired through our thinking and research into the outer sense world. We can impose a certain resignation, a certain renunciation upon ourselves, we can learn at such points not to want to judge the supersensible with what we have learned and experienced in the sense world.

It is here that the main obstacles lie for most people in entering upon the science of spirit. They see the limits of knowledge but they do not then have the courage to renounce or resign. They do not say that they cannot try to enter into the spiritual world with what they have learned and experienced in the sense world, but they try to penetrate beyond these limits, even if only in a negative sense, by using the kind of concepts and ideas acquired in studying the sense world. The one person does it by constructing all sorts of hypotheses about what could exist in the supersensible, the other by rejecting the supersensible completely on the basis of his study of the sense world; in other words, taking upon himself the capacity to make judgments about the supersensible with the concepts he has acquired from the sense world. Those also have not understood the experience of the border-areas of knowledge who, like materialists, monists and the like, begin to decide that nothing exists beyond the sense world on the basis of the ideas and concepts acquired through the life of the senses.

This is the point where something quite special must arise within human soul life, where what I have just characterized, this renunciation of the concepts acquired through living in the sense-world, where we do not just wish to make a statement or bring something intellectual and logical to expression, but that this renunciation becomes an inner intellectual virtue, something that—if I may be excused the phrase—cuts into human soul life, so that at certain points we really acquire a subtle feeling that we should not proceed further with what we have learned in the sense-world. For if this renunciation is not just a logical admission or an intellectual conclusion, but an inner virtue, then this virtue arising out of the renunciation radiates toward the inner life of the soul, and then what we have renounced outwardly is taken up into the inner life of the soul. The renunciation makes us fit for undertaking in course of time the two spiritual functions necessary to penetrate from the sphere of the soul in human experience into the spiritual world. For this two inner functions are necessary, but which, as you can see from my book, *Knowledge of the Higher Worlds and its Attainment,* involve many individual functions and exercises, which are contained in these two main aims, for which there are two main functions. The first is that we achieve real self observation; the second consists in striving to experience the soul-spirit sphere that is no longer dependent on the bodily nature, but proceeds purely in the spirit. However paradoxical it may appear to present-day humanity, it must nevertheless be said that this second function consists in the human being forming his soul-spirit life in such a way that when he investigates the spirit, his soul-spirit experience is no longer in the body, but outside it. This is no doubt something that appears quite ridiculous to those who think they keep firmly within the province of the scientific outlook. But the science of spirit will bring home to people that many of our ideas will have to be changed, even into the opposite of what we are accustomed to, just as the Copernican outlook meant a complete reversal in the way people thought about the relationship of the planets to the sun.

What is normally called self-observation, an introversion of the soul, is not what is meant by true self-observation by the science of spirit. It is true that one can start from this brooding in oneself in order to find the way one has to go toward true self-observation, but real self-observation has to be taken in hand much more seriously and much more energetically. For it includes something which even earnest psychologists maintain is impossible. I have already pointed out in earlier lectures that when philosophers speak about the human soul they find it characteristic that in certain respects the life of the soul is not able to observe itself. They point out that if we have learned a poem by heart and then wish to recite it, but at the same time observing ourselves as we recite, we begin to falter and interrupt ourselves. It is not possible to carry out something and at the same time stand by and observe ourselves. This is cited as being something characteristic of the human soul, that it cannot do this. Now it must be said that those who find that this is in fact so, that it is impossible, will not get anywhere with the science of spirit, because this "impossibility" is just what the scientist of spirit has to achieve. The ability or capacity which is brought to our notice in normal life when we observe ourselves reciting and make ourselves falter, this ability has to be acquired by the scientist of spirit. We have to be able to split our soul-life wide open so that we can observe scientifically what we ourselves do. It is not all that important to learn a poem to achieve this, although this is one way of doing it, providing we do the necessary practice, and it is also good preparation for the real exercise of self-observation if we do it. It is a form of preparation to achieve reciting a poem with all its shades of feeling sufficiently automatically—if I may use such a crude expression—that we do not interrupt ourselves when we observe ourselves while reciting. The important thing, however, is not to concentrate on the outer aspects, but to apply such activity to the life of the soul itself. This means that we have to observe how one thought follows another, our thinking and imaginative life, so that at the same time we can allow the thought processes to proceed while on the other hand we can observe them in full consciousness. It would lead too far now to describe how this is done, but you can read about it in my books, *Knowledge of Higher Worlds and its Attainment,* in *Riddles of Man,* and similar books. It is absolutely possible to achieve real self-observation in this way. It is not then a mere intellectual process, but it is something real, for it is a first beginning of the emergence of the spirit-nature out of the soul-nature. The experience of the soul is observed by the spirit which has really tried to separate itself from the soul-nature. But this is only one aspect of what can be observed.

Now it is necessary to add that renouncing entering the supersensible with the concepts and according to the laws taken from the sense world becomes a virtue and permeates the entire life of the soul, and when this has happened it not only produces the kind of modesty we are used to from normal life, but it produces an inward, intellectual modesty and humility which make us suited in the first place to exercising self-observation of the kind I have just been speaking about. We are not intimately organized enough, as it were, to be able to carry out such self-observation until we have radiated this intellectual virtue over our own souls.

But, on the other hand, something else is necessary. What then is attained when we achieve such self-observation? What is achieved when self-observation is practiced is that what normally disturbs the human being when he carries out a soul function is taken in hand, and our will is strengthened and driven out of the sphere of the soul into the sphere of the spirit. Then there is something further that has to be striven for: the will itself has to take on a new direction, has to acquire a new mode of activity in the soul. This can happen only if the human being does not employ the will as he normally does in ordinary life in carrying out outward functions, but if he employs it in carrying out inner functions. In living in his sense perception and in the ideas and images derived from these perceptions, the human being is accustomed in the way and sequence in which his thoughts are constructed to being led by the sense world. He allows one thought to follow another because he first experiences one event in the sense world, then a second one, and so on.

The human being allows his thoughts to follow the sequence of outer events and in ordinary life he hardly ever gets used to leading his will into his thought life, into the inner processes of his soul, which are to be perceived just by this true self-observation. But this he has to do if he is to become a scientist of spirit. He has to try—for a long time, energetically and patiently—to lead his will into his thinking and power of imagination. Again and again he has to try to carry out a process of the soul which in an objective and genuine sense can be called meditating, an inner reflection, though not a dreamy, mystical reflection, but one which represents a real process in the inner life, so that the will is really led into the thinking. Whereas we are normally accustomed to arranging our ideas according to outer events, we endeavor in moments set aside for the purpose, to formulate ideas whose sequence is determined solely by the inner will working according to a much greater view of life. We guide the will into our life of images and ideas. In this way we come to recognize what sort of relationship can exist between the inner will of man and his life of images and ideas. We do not become acquainted with this at all in our normal consciousness. In order to make this point perfectly clear, I would like to give the following illustration. Imagine a person living in a semi-sleeping state in dreams. He knows full well that these dreams are pictures passing before his soul according to certain laws. These pictures surge to and fro. Because they appear, so far as normal life is concerned, as dream pictures, the human being cannot control them with his will. If in his semi-sleeping state he were able to pull himself together to such an extent that he could control the sequence of dream pictures, he would then more or less be in the position I have been talking about, where our own will controls the ideas and images we ourselves make.

But this is not the point that matters ultimately. Everything we have discussed so far is only a preparatory exercise. For we naturally do not arrive at anything real only by the inner will controlling the sequence of ideas, which we know are not remembered, but arise out of the body. We do not arrive at anything special by piecing together ideas we have made, and can survey. But we do attain something when we set to work on the exercises with the mood which makes the renunciation into an intellectual virtue. Then we gradually notice something quite special in the life of the soul. And I may be allowed to say that what I have to say here about the science of spirit, by means of which we can really penetrate into spiritual spheres and which should be imagined as already having attained a certain development, and which also empowers one to say something about the spiritual world, that it should not be thought that it is like maintaining that natural science has its strict method which takes years to learn, and now the science of spirit comes along and talks about such inner ideas and images. This is not the case. Those who have acquainted themselves with biology and physiology, and know about their scientific methods and have then taken up the science of spirit know that however difficult it may be and that however much patience is demanded over the years by scientific method, significant results can be experienced in the science of spirit only if even more patience and even more work, even when this work is purely spiritual, are employed. Years of inner work are necessary to achieve anything of any consequence that can penetrate into the spiritual world, work which has been characterized as the leading of the will into our thought life by means of the inner functions or exercises which you can find in the above-mentioned books. We only have to know the one *and* the other to realize that the seriousness of the one is not inferior to the seriousness of the other. But what is important is not that we do the exercises, but that we achieve what we are able to achieve by means of the mood of renunciation. And we gradually notice that it is not our will alone, not the will which we have led into our thinking and imagination, that lives in what happens in our souls, but something else lives in them.

In our observation of the outer world we see how one event follows another, how one object is related to another, and how the sequence of our ideas follows what we see, follows the thread of outer events. Now we discover what it is that permits one idea to arise out of another, what it is that ensures that we do not add just any soul experience to another, but order such experiences according to an inner process. We discover a continual current in the life of the soul. Just as outer sense-nature is inner physical nature, so spiritual nature lives in the life of the soul. Whoever believes that we can still act arbitrarily or out of prejudice does not know this inner necessity. It is just as much a necessity as is necessity in ordinary life, and it fashions an inner, spiritual experience just as our ordinary experience comes to us by necessity according to the course of events in the physical world.

One who has had to do with the science of spirit for decades may well be allowed to speak of his experience, and this is, that this experience reveals what it is like through its own nature, its own character; arbitrariness ceases, and it is the spirit that orders the sequence of soul experiences. This comes to light when we set out to penetrate a particular sphere of the spiritual world with assumptions, acquired according to our images of the sense world, that spiritual beings or processes have to behave in a particular way. In countless cases—and this is so significant, so incisive for a true scientist of spirit—we experience that things turn out to be quite different from what we had expected, having formed a judgment according to the standards of the outer sense world. It transpires that on this path once we have grasped the inward spiritual necessity, we achieve results that cannot in any way be imagined on the basis of what we know from the sense world, because as far as the sense world is concerned they are quite contradictory. In experiencing this, which can in no way be compared to anything in the sense world, we know what it means to say that the spirit, which we have discovered, orders the sequence of our soul experiences just as our ideas which we formulate about the outer sense world are ordered according to the physical sequence of events.

And these two things come together: what we have acquired in inner strength by means of true self-observation, and what we have acquired of the objective course of the spirit, which is like the course of the outer sense-world. These come together and lead the human soul into a region of the spirit to which it belongs with its spiritual organs, just as the ordinary scientist is led into the bodily organization when he proceeds from hunger to non-physical processes in the body. When we use the soul as the starting point for investigating the spirit, certain phenomena of human soul life take on a new aspect. When the scientist of spirit is touched in this way by the real form, the real character, of the spirit, certain phenomena of human soul life become quite different. This happens, above all, when, by means of the spiritual nature he has acquired through self-observation, the human being has come to recognize the spiritual which gives direction to the soul life. It is only then that he is able to formulate a true idea, a true concept, of what we call the ego of the human being, which bestows as much of the spirit on the human soul as is bestowed of the body on normal human consciousness by the visible form and physiognomy. We cannot investigate the ego by philosophising about it, but only by making the will into thinking and the thinking into an act of will. By means of self-observation the will becomes an instrument of thinking and the thinking an instrument of will. This is a 'change of spirit' rather like the change of matter which is sought and found in the physical world in our digestion. We then approach the ego not by philosophising, speculation or hypotheses, but we first acquire a real spiritual observation of the ego and are only then in a position to formulate a correct view of it. This correct view of it proves to us that it is impossible to achieve such a view of the ego in ordinary life, in our ordinary consciousness. The picture which this ordinary consciousness (which is also prevalent in natural science) has of the ego, is that the latter gradually evolves as the body grows. A child does not appear to have an ego. As the body develops and gradually acquires its proper configuration the ego appears to wrestle its way out of the body. This view is held as a matter of course, and with the normal outlook of today it is not possible to arrive at any other view. And this is just what one has to achieve as a scientist of spirit— that one has to give the ordinary outlook its due in its own sphere and not become intolerant because one realizes that only one view is possible in the sphere in which materialism can operate.

In achieving spiritual observation and observation of the ego it is possible to see where the error of the ordinary outlook lies. It can be characterized in the following way. If we reflect about the relationship of the lungs to the air, we know that lungs and air belong together. But because in this case ordinary observation suffices to ascertain the true relationship, no one knowing things only from a superficial viewpoint would come to any other view than that air comes from outside, penetrates into the lungs, is then breathed out of the lungs and returns to the atmosphere outside. Because this kind of observation suffices, no one could maintain that the lung itself creates the air, that the air which is breathed out somehow has its origin in the lung itself, that the lung produces air. Our ordinary observation gives us insight into the relationship of the lungs to the air. Likewise our higher, spiritual observation gives us insight into the human ego. When we can use this observation which I have described, we know that the human ego is no more connected to the bodily nature, that is, to everything we have inherited from our father and mother, than the air which comes from outside has to do with the lungs. We get to know the ego as it really is and we know that in taking over what is inherited at birth or conception, in a sense it inhales out of the spiritual world. As a mass of air that at a particular moment is in our lungs, has flowed in from outside, so the ego flows out of the spiritual world into the bodily nature, out of the world in which it existed before the body could even be thought of in terms of conception and birth. Likewise, when the human being goes through the gate of death it flows out again, just as air which has been used up by the body flows out again from the lungs. We get to know the connection of the ego to a spiritual world that is independent of the world of the human body, just as in physics we learn about the connection of air to a greater mass of air which is independent of the human lung. This is how we rise to real knowledge of the ego, and it is the first thing we come to know about the nature of the ego. From this point we learn more and more by intensifying our spiritual observation by means of the methods described in the above-mentioned books. We learn about the ego as something independent of the life of the body in the same way that we learn about the body by using hunger and thirst as our starting points for investigating the chemical and physical processes of the body with physical methods. Only we discover the spiritual, which gives us our first view of the ego, as a state where the ego is embedded in spiritual beings. In order to know the physical body in all its aspects, we divide it into its various members. In a similar way we have to link the ego to other spiritual beings, which can be observed by spiritual observation with the methods I have described. The ego is linked to them and we find a complete ego-organism. This then extends beyond the individual life of the body.

Starting from the ego, from the part of our soul life that is directed toward the ego, we find that it is embedded in a spiritual life that exists before birth and continues after the gate of death is passed through. In the spiritual world we find a soul-spirit world that in the first instance is independent of the physical world. The ego belongs to this soul-spirit world. The first entities that we find there are spirit-soul beings with whom the ego of man is connected, beings that are human souls before or after death, with whom the human being is himself connected, and also other beings. When we observe the sense world we find a kingdom below man, the animal kingdom. In the soul-spirit world we find first of all a sphere to which the human ego belongs, which it fits into organically, where it performs its transformation of spirit, its spiritual digestion—a spirit-soul sphere which in the first instance is of a purely spirit-soul nature. Then we find a sphere ranking above this one, just as the animal kingdom ranks above the plant kingdom, and it ranks higher because in these higher spheres beings are to be found which are not only connected to us in our soul and spirit nature, in our inner life, but which are still more powerful because they bring about the harmony existing between the spirit-soul and the physical-bodily nature. For our spirit-soul nature has to be brought into relationship with our physical-bodily nature. This relationship is brought about by higher spiritual beings than we first meet.

Having made a start with spiritual investigation, we should not hesitate to speak about these real, concrete, spirit-soul beings that we really discover. The spiritual regions are discovered in which the ego performs its transformation of spirit, just as the physical kingdoms are discovered when we direct our attention to the animals, plants and minerals. And we discover further where lies the mystery of the soul entering and leaving the body. For we come to know how the relationship of the ego to the body of the human being works.

Here, it is true, we are entering a sphere which is quite remote from the present-day outlook, but which in future will have to become more and more a part of this outlook. If we observe the ego in this way we find it is related with the spirit-soul beings of the higher spiritual spheres, which range above the purely natural spheres. But in the trans-formation of spirit, which is analogous to the transfor-mation of matter in digestion, the ego undergoes a certain process. To begin with, it can only be associated with spirit-soul beings. This is the case before birth and after death, where it has a purely spiritual being for its organization and this is linked to the rest of the spirit world. As the ego proceeds through the spirit world, as it develops in the spirit world, it increasingly acquires a self-orientation and becomes gradually separated from the spirit world. The picture we have of the ego from the science of spirit is that long before birth or after death it has a special connection to many, many spiritual beings. Then as its development proceeds, it separates itself off and becomes in a sense dependent upon itself. It is in undergoing this separation and limitation that it evolves the power of attraction toward the bodily nature. This power of attraction impels it to unite itself—as the air unites itself to the lungs—with the bodily nature that arises in the course of human generations as a result of heredity. The ego enters into this when it comes from the spirit world.

Thus we gain a true view of the eternal working within the bodily nature of man, within the human being as a whole, not by philosophical speculation, but by laying bare this eternal, by entering into the eternal ourselves with our souls. This is the way spiritual observation works. We must be quite sure to realize that everything I have described— the striving for self-observation, the striving to guide the will into our thought and imaginative life, the striving to attain the transformation of spirit—that all this is really only a preparation. Everything else has to be waited for. Just as we have to wait for what the sense world speaks to us when it approaches the soul from outside, so we have to wait for what the spirit-world speaks to us. Self-observation, the guidance of the will into the thought and imaginative life, these have to be striven for in order to prepare the soul to experience the spirit. Spiritual life then begins, but it has to penetrate toward the sphere of the soul and of the spirit.

Thus I have outlined the ways which lead us to see our real soul life in thinking, feeling and willing as an expression of the spiritual, just as hunger, thirst and the need to breathe are an expression in the soul of what lives in the body. This then leads to the differentiation of the eternal-spiritual from the soul nature.

Tomorrow we shall have to describe how something of the eternal in the human being finds its way into ordinary consciousness as a revelation of the unconscious. My intention today was to show how we rise from the sphere of the soul to the spirit. This description, which is a description of knowledge gained by the science of spirit, appears, it is true, to be paradoxical to the normally accepted concepts of today. But you will perhaps have seen that the science of spirit takes its science just as seriously as does natural science. Natural science leads to the perishable and transitory, the science of spirit leads to the eternal, to the imperishable, without which the perishable can, in fact, be explained. Thus we can say that from the vantage point of the science of spirit we are able to have an overall view of what is portrayed in natural science. It is only then that we can really appreciate the value of natural science, and are then in a position to judge it. If we get no further than natural science we arrive at the judgment or belief that a stringent science is only possible within the sense world, that it cannot rise to the eternal. If we take up the science of spirit, we know why the natual scientist has to say this if he does not get beyond the position of natural science. But by developing our normal consciousness, by laying bare the spiritual forces slumbering in the soul, we recognize that man can penetrate into the eternal of his own being, into what is really immortal in himself, for this immortal part of him, in fact, makes its own existence known itself. The red color of the rose does not have to be proved. The spirit in us that goes through birth and death also testifies to its own existence when we are able to observe it.

Anyone basing his observation on the science of spirit has an overall view of natural science as well, and he also gives the latter its due. He does not do what those who follow only natural science do, who—consciously or unconsciously—undo what the science of spirit does and wish to take the ground away from under its feet. We may well say that the scientist of spirit has nothing to be afraid of. He need not fear the objections which come from various quarters, for he knows what these objections are worth, and can also recognize why they have to be made. He is quite justified in thinking that he does not need to try to prevent someone from recognizing the methods and progress of natural science. On the contrary. The scientist of spirit is able to say to someone wishing to go into natural science: Go your way to natural science and if you do not only look at it with the eyes of the natural scientific outlook, but with the eyes of the spiritual way of investigation, you will not only find no contradiction between natural science and the science of spirit, but you will also find everywhere in natural science the confirmation and revelation of what the science of spirit says. And we should not believe that the scientist of spirit has any wish to prevent those whom he addresses from following any particular religious confession. It is the greatest misunderstanding of all to believe that we wish to set up any sort of religious gulf between a religious approach and the science of spirit. Dr. Rittelmeyer has shown quite clearly in an admirable article in *Christliche Welt* how in a quite objective way the science of spirit can be a foundation for religious life, that it does not take anyone away from true religious life, but, on the contrary, leads them toward it.

The science of spirit does not need to keep people away from religious life. Just as it can say: go to natural science in order to realize what the science of spirit is, so it can also say: go to religion, come to know religion, experience religion, and you will find that what the science of spirit is able to give to the soul gives religious life its foundation and strengthens it.

Go out into life itself and you will find that the concepts given in the science of spirit do not deaden you to life or make you unfit for life, but that they make the spirit mobile, agile, and place the human being into life, ready for action. Practical life, too, will be a confirmation and proof of what the science of spirit is able to give to the human being.

Because natural science has to keep to its own course, has

to direct its attention solely to nature and may not mix nature with anything of soul and spirit, it is imperative for the science of spirit to find its place alongside it as equally justified. The science of spirit must penetrate from the soul to the spirit, just as natural science has to penetrate from the soul to the physical body. The time will then come when the real essence, the real basic concept of the science of spirit, will be understood, when the intentions of the scientists—to take the ground away from the science of spirit—will be seen in their true light. Forty or fifty years ago Dubois-Reymond was able to say: "Science ends where the supersensible begins." In the future this saying will be confronted by another arising out of the spiritual scientific view: What was really happening when natural science wanted to formulate a system of thought, a view of the world that is supersensible, when it restricted itself to nature above? In a sense one could see that there is something that surrounds the human being in his existence and in which he has his roots, that comes from a particular origin. One saw it rooted in the spirit, but could not penetrate into this spirit.

The science of spirit shows how we can penetrate into spiritual life. The kind of position which natural science has occupied regarding the spirit—if I may use the comparison —is rather as if one were to see a tree which has its roots in the ground. The tree cannot be seen entirely, for the roots are in the ground. The tree is then dug up in order to see it in its entirety, for nothing of the tree may remain hidden. The tree will dry up and will no longer be able to flourish.—This is what has been done by the scientific outlook. It has dug up the being of man out of its foundations in order to acquire an overall view. The resulting view is then like the tree that has been taken out of the ground. The tree has to wither away, and the life that arises out of this view of the world has to wither away. Once this is realized, the way to the science of spirit will be found.

In order to acquire an overall view, the being of man has been deprived of its roots. For the sake of life, for the sake of real life, the human being will once again be immersed in what is popularly called the unconscious, but which, when it is revealed in the sphere of consciousness, can be raised into the sphere of real knowledge of the supersensible. Then the time will come when the view will be firmly implanted in the human mind that the eternal core of man's being is rooted in the spirit and that if we want to get to know the human being in his entirety we have to penetrate to the spirit. Then it will no longer be said, as Dubois-Reymond did, that science cannot find the supersensible, not even in its simplest form of manifestation, that this is where science stops, but the science of the future will say that all science that is not rooted in the supersensible will not be in a position to explain existence, will not be able to lead us into the life of existence, but will only be able to kill existence. It will not be said that science ends where supra-naturalism, the supersensible, begins, but, the life of science ends where the human being no longer takes his stand in the supersensible, and the death of science enters where the supersensible is abandoned.

The Psychological Expression of the Unconscious

I took the liberty of pointing out yesterday that there is some antipathy on the part of the ordinary scientific outlook toward the nature and the entire method of the science of spirit which can and must be placed alongside ordinary science. I pointed out further that there is a certain subjective prejudice at the present time which makes it difficult for people really to go into and acquire an understanding of the science of spirit, that is, for people who think they stand on the sure foundation of science — on which, of course, the science of spirit also stands — but who are of the opinion that it is not possible to bridge the gap from this kind of foundation to a real science of spirit. However, a fact about the soul-life of present day humanity emerged from my exposition yesterday, the fact that it is just in immersing ourselves in the scientific knowledge of the present time that we are bound to long, and indeed, do long to acquire knowledge about the human being that goes beyond the ordinary everyday life of the soul, which, of course, of necessity is tied to the observation and experience of the physical sense world.

Now it is naturally possible to say that the views of the world generally held, that have arisen through the influence of scientific ideas, are proving to be increasingly incapable of dealing with methods of research other than those which are concerned with what is physically present in the world. And so now it is intended to investigate what lies beyond normal consciousness with the same kind of sense perception — providing we really do want to investigate it, and not just drop it — as science uses to investigate nature. For this reason the existence of one border area at least in human experience has found recognition recently among people who want their work to remain on a scientific basis but who, on the other hand, desire to penetrate the mysteries of human soul life, inasmuch as this lies within the conscious sphere that is, as I have said, more or less tied to the world of the senses. People have gradually become convinced that it is not possible to investigate the mysteries of soul life, that there is much that rises up into the soul life of the human being out of unknown depths, or one could also say, out of unknown heights, that is well suited to provide information about what the core of man's being really is, rather than what is to be found within our ordinary consciousness. But because, generally speaking, the science of spirit is regarded as something not sufficiently tangible, as something that leads one away from the real world—so many would say—an attempt is made to investigate a kind of border area by ordinary scientific means.

The science of spirit has therefore every reason from its point of view, to refer to this border area and to deal with it. It is the region that we have more recently become accustomed to call the unconscious. There is also another reason why it is especially important for the science of spirit to offer some thoughts about this area of the unconscious, and that is because some of the things that are said in this connection are misunderstood, so that the science of spirit is confused with what is said about this border area, more or less justifiably, by those representing other approaches to the problem. By "unconscious" one usually means what rises up from unknown regions and flows into one's conscious life. It would of course take a very long time if I were even to give an outline of all that science over the whole world has had to say about this region of the unconscious. In the cultural life of Central Europe the expression "the unconscious" has of course become well known since the 1860's through the popular philosophy of Eduard von Hartmann, who sought the reasons for all that the human being experiences consciously in a spiritual unconscious, whether it be below or above the conscious.

If I may be allowed, by way of introduction, to make a personal remark — the way in which Eduard von Hartmann approaches spiritual life, which is supposed to remain unconscious for ordinary consciousness (although he is dealing with something spiritual and although he sees a revelation of the unconscious, of the spiritual unconscious, in the physical sense world), his approach and outlook are in a way diametrically opposed to the view which I am putting forward. And through being personally acquainted with Eduard von Hartmann I tried already in the 1880's to thrash these things out with him personally and in correspondence. I tried to show the difference between the anthroposophically orientated science of spirit and an outlook founded on the unconscious like, for instance, that of Eduard von Hartmann. I discussed this difference recently in a rather personal way in the February number of the second year of the magazine *Das Reich*. I shall now indicate in a few words what is discussed more fully there:

Eduard von Hartmann points out that everything the human being is able to reveal in his ordinary life rests on something spiritual and unconscious. He maintains the view that this unconscious can be reached only by means of the power of logical thinking; it deduces something unknown that abides, that can be reached only conceptually and grasped in hypotheses from what is perceptible in the sense world. And he points out that this unconscious is not in itself conscious in the same way that the human being, for instance, is conscious. — In these two respects the science of spirit is radically different from this view of Eduard von Hartmann: firstly the science of spirit is founded on the fact that — I described this more fully yesterday and named the books which provide the necessary basis — it not only seeks to penetrate the spiritual spheres by means of hypotheses and logical deductions, but by bringing out of the soul certain forces that slumber in it which remain unconscious for our ordinary consciousness, forces that are raised into our consciousness by means of a strengthening and intensification of our soul life. These unconscious forces in the soul are able to enter into the consciousness of the human being, so that he can tread the path from the sense world to the supersensible world in full consciousness by means of spiritual observation, so that he can observe this supersensible world in a spiritual way, just as he can observe the sense world. The science of spirit, therefore, does not describe a hypothetical path from the sense world into the supersensible, but a real path that can be experienced. And on the other hand, the science of spirit has to emphasize that something spiritual that is unconscious, in which no consciousness can be found, is really of no more value than the great unconscious sphere of purely material atoms and their processes, the purely physical foundation of existence. What would be the point of something spiritual that is supposed to underlie the sense world, if it is unconscious? For then the human being would be the only conscious being to raise himself out of a world, which, as far as consciousness is concerned, would have no more value than the unconscious world of purely material phenomena? — The science of spirit, therefore, does not deal with this unconscious, which in itself is devoid of consciousness, but is concerned with spiritual beings existing behind the physical world and which are just as conscious as human beings, and in some respects even have a higher consciousness than the latter.

This is what differentiates the view of the anthroposophically orientated science of spirit about the unconscious from such a view as Eduard von Hartmann's, which is actually held by many people today in the same sense as he held it, even if they do not intend getting away from the scientific viewpoint.

Today we shall have opportunity to show in what way the

science of spirit can really penetrate into the sphere of spiritual life, and we shall do this by taking into consideration the unconscious phenomena in human soul life which enter into our consciousness in a less complete way than does the science of spirit.

But I must take certain things for granted, which were described yesterday — that by means of inner processes in the soul (if we wish to be particular, we should call them "exercises") our ordinary soul life, even if it is only a mystical soul life, can be treated in such a way that the human being can rise from this soul life to the spiritual, just as from another aspect he can descend from soul life to the physical by means of scientific observation. Having acquired this perception of the spiritual or — to use Goethe's expression once more — the eyes of the spirit and the ears of the spirit, we are then in a position to view what normally appears in our conscious soul life from unknown depths or heights from our newly-won viewpoint in a quite different way.

Now of course the border areas with which we are concerned cover a wide field. Today I shall select only a few of them, but they will shed light on everything else in our unconscious soul life and its manifestations. I shall take something which is well known to everyone, but which remains an enigma in human existence: our world of dreams. I shall then deal with a subject that more recently has become the child of all those who seek to penetrate into the spiritual supersensible world, but who shy away from practising the real science of spirit; and that child is what is called "somnambulism" and also "mediumship," which is related to it. I shall then proceed to another aspect where it is certainly sufficiently well known that it arises out of the unconscious depths of soul life, and this is the whole sphere of artistic enjoyment and creation, which I shall deal with briefly. Then I shall come to a subject which perhaps many people do not consider belongs to the unconscious and its manifestation, but which at least can be seen — by those who are reasonable about it — to be something that plays into our semiconscious life, and this is the sphere of human destiny, which will be considered from the viewpoint of the science of spirit, the real and true clairvoyance. I am not fond of the word clairvoyance because it is mixed up with all sorts of amateurish and other nonsense, but the way I use it today will perhaps be justified, and should be self-explanatory. I shall indicate what is the sphere of the science of spirit itself, for this science feels itself called upon to raise what is spiritually unconscious into consciousness.

I would like first of all to describe one or two characteristic properties of the real experience the scientist of the spirit has of the supersensible, spiritual world. This will then form the basis for what I have to say about the other phenomena of the unconscious, which I have so far only just mentioned and which I shall describe later from the viewpoint of the science of spirit. As we have not much time, I shall not be able to go into the ordinary scientific view of these things as well.

When the human soul has reached the point with the scientist of spirit of being able to approach a spiritual world in the same way that we approach the physical sense world with our physical eyes and ears and the other sense organs, then the human being perceives the spiritual world and can grasp its connection with the physical sense world.

I pointed out yesterday that it is quite unjustified to object that what the science of spirit describes is really only put together out of the physical sense world and then transferred to the spiritual world. And I also pointed out that anyone who has conscientiously used the methods of the science of spirit for several years knows that he often finds himself in the position that what he experiences in the spiritual world looks quite different from anything that can be experienced in the transistory physical sense world. Even in the experience of the spiritual world, the whole mood and constitution of the soul is radically different from normal soul life. And so I would like first of all to describe one or two characteristic properties of this experience in the spirit.

If one has only a superficial understanding of what we mean by the science of spirit it is easy enough to say that the scientist of spirit lives in a kind of self-deception: — he puts things together in his mind and thinks that the resulting idea is the revelation of a spiritual world, having overlooked or forgotten how he really gained the idea through sense perception in the first place. — Of course, it is true that if the scientist of spirit were to experience spiritual perception in the same way he gains ideas from the sense world, then he would naturally become suspicious of the science of spirit. But this is not the case. One of the most fundamental characteristics of what we are able to perceive in our thoughts of the sense world appears quite different when compared with real spiritual experiences. The ideas and images we form through contact with the sense world are impressed upon the soul, and we are able to recall them after a while; they can be raised up out of the treasure of our memory. The spiritual experiences which the scientist of spirit has are different, for it is not possible to recall them in this way. What the soul experiences when it approaches spiritual perception is not just an idea. For an idea can be incorporated into the memory, but a spiritual experience of this sort cannot be directly incorporated into the soul. A spiritual experience or perception disappears, just as our view of a tree that we have looked at for a time disappears when we turn away from it. When the perception comes to an end, it can no longer be experienced by the soul — we have to approach it again in order to see it as it really is. The image or idea we keep in our memory, but to see the actual tree we have to go to where it is. Just as we no longer see the tree when we have gone away from it, so the spiritual perception is no longer experienced by the soul when the perception itself has ceased. From this it follows that with experience of a spiritual nature we are not dealing with a mere combination of ideas, thoughts and images, for they can be remembered.

But then one could object that if this is in fact the case, it would never be possible to report such spiritual experience if it could not be remembered — nothing could be said about it, for it would disappear from our soul life as soon as it had been experienced. — But actually it is not like this at all. The scientist of spirit can formulate ideas about what he has experienced spiritually, just as we are able to formulate ideas about things, beings and processes in the sense world, and these ideas can be retained. It depends on the scientist of spirit being able to differentiate actual experience from the images and ideas which arise out of it, just as in ordinary life we distinguish our sense perception from the idea which arises from it. We can look at this in another way. If we wish to have a spiritual experience in the same way a second or third time, it is not sufficient just to recall the image or idea of it. For in this case it is clear that we do not then have the full experience, but only a pale image of it.

If we want to have the experience again, we have to reawaken the slumbering forces of the soul and to enter into the experience afresh. With certain characteristic phenomena of the spiritual world we can only remember the way we approached the experience — this can be recalled, and the experience attained a second, third or fourth time. But then it is certainly not a case of the experience following the same laws that underlie the normal way of imagining and thinking. — This is the one aspect. You can see from this that the scientist of spirit is no dreamer, but that his own inner self-perception enables him to be absolutely clear about what leads him to real experiences.

The second aspect is that an experience attained through the science of spirit has a relationship to our soul life quite different from an experience that takes place in our normal consciousness in the physical sense world. What would be the use of our physical life if we were not able to acquire certain skills, certain habits, if we were not in a position of being able to try and do something better a second time, when the repetition of an action would serve no purpose? The repetition of an action is incorporated into our normal experience as a habit. But spiritual experiences cannot be incorporated into our soul life in the same way. Many — those who are beginners in spiritual experience — find this out, to their surprise. It is comparatively easy — I say comparatively easy — to achieve certain initial experiences of the spiritual world if one carries out the exercises described in my book *How to Attain Knowledge of Higher Worlds,* and beginners are always overjoyed when they have their first experiences of a spiritual nature. But then they are all the more surprised when these experiences cannot easily be repeated, or when they cannot be repeated at all. And one can feel very miserable because an experience which one has had cannot be recalled; one does not seem to get any better at it. It is not possible to turn what has been experienced in the spirit into a habit. On the contrary, with repetition it becomes increasingly more difficult to do the repetition. Thus, as a matter of fact, a large part of the exercises that have to be done if we wish to bring about a repetition of certain experiences, consists of doing quite different things the second or third time. Experience of a spiritual nature has therefore a quite different relationship to the physical, since it works against habit.

There is a third aspect of what is characteristic in spiritual experience, and that is, however odd it may sound, that real spiritual experience — which has absolutely nothing to do with anything concerned with the body — is something that is over in a split second. In fact, this is even a reason why so few people today attain spiritual experience. In ordinary life people are accustomed to take a certain time to assimilate something that appears on their horizon. If the experience is a spiritual one, it is over before the person has been able to notice it. What is therefore necessary above all in order to have real spiritual experience, is what one could call presence of mind. If we want to have spiritual experience we have to get used to situations in ordinary life which demand quick decisions, where the situation must be summed up immediately, and where there is no time to delay by changing our minds. People who have no wish to make any progress in this kind of self-education, to make quick decisions in certain situations, to see quickly what has to be done, are not suited to gaining the necessary control over their own souls in order to achieve spiritual experience easily. The kind of person who can tackle a situation, not by looking at it from every possible angle and fussing about, but by making a decision immediately upon being confronted with the situation and then also sticking to it, has a good foundation for spiritual experience. For spiritual experiences within us have to be gone through just as quickly as we have to grasp some situations in life and make decisions, which if they were not made quickly would perhaps lead to misfortune and ruin. — I am not saying that spiritual experience can lead to ruin, for in this case it will not have existed. This attitude toward it is necessary.

And now there is a fourth characteristic — that spiritual experiences are always individual. In the physical world we are accustomed to dividing everything into particular classes or categories, in fact we divide the whole of life in this way. We speak of the famous — if not notorious — "Scheme F." Everything has to belong to a certain category, to be put in its particular place. People believe that law is to be found in the world of phenomena only when everything is fitted into various categories. We should imagine for once how we should deal with nature, which we quite rightly divide into categories, if everything were individual. And we should imagine what human life would be like if it were not, for instance, possible in every single instance to turn to a book of laws, if it were not possible to fit a particular case neatly into a ready-made compartment, but if we had to face it with individual judgment. People are accustomed from experience in the physical world to making everything fit into patterns. All this putting things into categories, classes, determining a particular order with particular laws, all this has to be given up, though not in connection with the physical world, for this would make one unfit for the latter, but for the sphere of spiritual experiences. What is experienced in the spiritual world is always portrayed as something individual. This is why people so often take a stand against the science of spirit. If we speak about what has been discovered by the science of spirit — and having given lectures for so many years now, I do not hesitate to present concrete examples about this science of spirit — let us say, for example, that I describe how the sudden death of a person has the effect in the spiritual world of his experiencing spiritually in the single moment when his physical body is destroyed through an accident, as much as he would have been able to experience in twenty or thirty years in life. If such a thing as this is described, then it can be related only to a particular case. Of course, someone else comes along and says, — Sudden deaths have this and that effect. He would like to make a law of it. Such laws, if I may put it this way, are the enemy of the true way of knowledge of the science of spirit, because in spiritual experience each single case represents something individual and unique, and because one always has to be surprised how something can always appear — and in life people like so much to stick to the old. One can write down the most subtle experiences of the physical world in a notebook and can put it in one's coat pocket. Such a procedure is impossible with knowledge derived from the science of spirit. This is why there are so many different kinds of descriptions that the scientist of spirit must give. Those of you who are here now and who have often been present at the lectures which have been given here for many years, will have heard me deal with similar subjects, never in the same way, but always varied in one way or the other, individualized. Last winter, for instance, I spoke on the same theme in many German cities, sometimes for several days in succession, but each time in a different way, describing the same things differently. Knowledge derived through the science of spirit makes a claim upon the spirit which we can describe as the mobility of this spirit. We conclude therefore that the important thing is not the content, the actual content of the words, but that this content is drawn and spoken out of the spirit itself.

You will see from this that it is always necessary to become accustomed to a quite different kind of mood and disposition of soul when we rise from the transitory to the intransitory, when we approach the part of man that belongs to the intransitory world, the eternal core of his being. It is therefore understandable that the science of spirit is not only considered to be difficult to understand, but is attacked, misunderstood and confused with all sorts of other things. As someone said recently (someone who prefers to hear only what he has heard before) — it is irritating. Of course it is irritating to someone who only wants all his old dogmas warmed up once again.

Thus it is not only that what the science of spirit has to say about the eternal, the spiritual, is different from what is to be found to be real in the physical sense world, but also that the attitude of the soul toward the spirit is different from its attitude toward the physical sense world. With the kind of attitude of soul I have just described in its characteristic properties, it is possible to approach the part of man that goes through births and deaths, the eternal core of the human being, which as a spiritual entity belongs to the spiritual world just as man as a physical, bodily creature belongs to physical nature and its kingdoms.

What the science of spirit finds in this way is at first something unconscious for our normal consciousness, but it can be drawn into our normal consciousness. This is the essential thing about the method of the science of spirit — that it sets out to reveal what in normal life is generally hidden in the unconscious of the human soul. For the science of spirit brings nothing new to light and does not invent it, but the eternal core of the human being goes through — to use yesterday's expression — a spiritual digestion, just as the physical body has a material digestion — this exists in every human being. The scientist of spirit only brings to light what functions and weaves within every human being. It is his task to bring to consciousness what otherwise remains unconscious. All he talks about is nothing other than the foundation out of which everyone speaks and thinks and acts. Only it so happens that the sphere of the spirit is either subconscious or superconscious — i. e. unconscious — for our normal consciousness.

Now, seen from the viewpoint of our normal soul life, something iridescent and vacillating enters into the sphere of this soul life. What is meant here belongs to the border areas which I have spoken about. Everyone is familiar with this border area which appears so ordinary and which yet is so mysterious : the remarkable sphere of our dream life. This dream life with its pictures that enters into our ordinary soul life, gives the investigator quite different problems from the person who just lets it pass him by, or at the most approaches it with a few superstitious ideas.

A lot could be said just to describe some of the more outward characteristics of our dream life, but here I only want to give a sketch of this dream life as seen by the science of spirit by calling special attention to a few of its characteristic properties — those properties which will serve to enable us to come to know the nature of it.

Presumably everyone knows—and many philosophical approaches to dreams have recognized this — that many of our dreams are stimulated by a sense impression. The world of dreams that we experience is very much connected with the world of our unconscious sleep. When a person is deep in unconscious sleep he is completely cut off from his environment, both by his senses and his limbs. If we are really in unconscious sleep there is nothing in the room, whatever may be there, that can affect our senses. We cannot think about anything that is around us, and in really dreamless sleep we are not able to do anything either. We can establish no relationship at all to our environment — in a sense we are isolated from what surrounds us. — What is characteristic of our dreams is that we really remain in a dreaming state in this isolation and even if the isolation appears to be broken by a sense impression, it is really only in appearance. What are such dreams? Everyone knows them. Someone dreams, for instance, about horses trotting by; he wakes up, and after waking knows exactly where the sound has come from — the ticking of a watch that he had put down nearby. He had heard this ticking because of a particularly sensitive functioning of his ears which must have started at that moment. But now what goes through the mind, the perception, does not work in the normal way as it would in the outer world, but in a dramatized form. Therefore we do not establish a relationship with our environment through our senses, but remain in an isolation which sleep has brought about, and what affects the senses is transformed in the soul. We dream, for example, of a red hot stove, we hear it roaring. — The beat of our heart has become stronger, and becomes the symbol in us of the roaring hot stove. We even have the same relationship to our body as we have in dreamless sleep; the soul simply transforms the impression that comes from the body. Thus we maintain the same relationship with our body when dreaming which we have in dreamless sleep — isolated even from our own body.

We all know that we go on whole journeys in dreams, journeys we could never undertake in real life, journeys where we fly with wings. But at the same time we know that all this does not change our relationship to the outer world, as it would do in real life. Even regarding what we experience as a relationship of our being to an environment in our dreams, nothing changes our relationship to the outer world.

So we can say that what is characteristic of dreams is that in an important respect they do not alter the relationship the human being has to his environment and to himself by virtue of his spirit-soul-body constitution operating through his senses, movements and his own physical body. This also distinguishes dreams from all the other unconscious regions I shall characterize today. It also distinguishes them from everything based on a change in the relationship of the human being to his environment. Even ordinary observation bears out the fact that dreams may not be confused with anything abnormal in soul experience, that they are quite normal and healthy, and are not abnormal in the way they appear in normal human soul life.

A peculiarity of dream life that is particularly important for what I am going to say is that the course of our dreams shows that we cease to join the sequence of dream images in a logical way. We are no longer connected to normal logic. We cannot be logical in dreams. There is one objection to this, however. — The scientist of spirit always knows the objections that can be made. Of course, the unfoldment of some dreams is such that we can say that the pictures are joined together in a logical sequence. But, in fact, it is different, for exact observation reveals that as long as a dream appears logical, it consists only of reminiscences of life, which had a logical sequence before. Whatever has a logical sequence in life can be dreamed again, but it does not become logical in the dream. The logic that is normally present in our soul life is therefore not present in the action of our dreams. Moral feelings and attitudes concerning human actions are also missing. We all know the many things we are capable of doing in dreams. We all know that in dreams we achieve things and ascribe them to ourselves, that we would condemn in ordinary life. Not only does logic come to an end in dreams, but our moral outlook as well. — These are two important characteristics that we must hold on to if we are to investigate the nature of dreams.

It is of course true that much can be said about dream life from the ordinary physical viewpoint, but we do not want to touch upon this today, for a merely outward scientific method of observation cannot get at the real nature of dreams — for the simple reason that there is nothing with which our normal consciousness can compare dream life. Dreams enter into our normal conscious experience as phenomena that cannot be compared with anything else. And if something cannot be compared with anything else, if it is not possible to incorporate it into a particular scheme, if it portrays something individual through its own particular nature, it cannot be studied by an external scientific method of observation. Only from the point of view of the science of spirit is it possible to gain a true picture of dreams and their nature, for the simple reason that by means of the development of the soul, which I have outlined today, the scientist of spirit attains a pictorial or other kind of spiritual experience which, while radically different from dreams, nevertheless in its form, experience, its intensity of experience, is somewhat similar to dreams. We can leave aside for the moment the question of how dreams are related to reality. We do not wish to go into this now. But the scientist of spirit knows that in what he experiences, which at first is pictorial, he stands before a real spiritual world, he experiences a spiritual world. He can therefore look at the world of dreams and describe it from the world he experiences. This is the one thing. By means of this he acquires a view given to him by his actual observation of what dreams really are in the human soul. Seen from the viewpoint of ordinary consciousness, it is not possible to know what dreams are. Dreams rise up in our soul life, surge up like unknown waves out of the depths, but we do not know what it is that is active, that is dreaming in our souls. But now the scientist of spirit, in practicing the activity necessary for spiritual investigation (as described yesterday), experiences another self, the same self, but in another form, the true ego — he experiences the spirit-soul nature of man independently of the bodily nature. However great a horror it may be for many people, it is nevertheless true that spiritual experiences are achieved outside the body. The scientist of spirit therefore knows what it means to be outside the body, and he can now compare this with the world of dreams. In seeing the world of dreams on the one hand, and knowing spiritual experiences on the other, he knows that the same thing that normally dreams in the soul is experienced spiritually when practising the science of spirit. It is one and the same thing: what dreams and what is active in the science of spirit, only in investigating the spirit we stand before the real region of the spirit, and in dreams — and this is what is important:— What is it that we stand before in dreams? The difference between standing before the reality of the spirit with our own self in the investigation of the spirit, and in our dreams, is that the scientist of spirit has prepared his soul beforehand to enter into the spiritual world, in which he then perceives in the same way that we normally perceive with our eyes and ears in the physical world, and through his investigation he discovers that in sleep the human being leaves the body. But because he lacks the necessary organs to perceive there, his consciousness remains dull and unconscious from the moment of going to sleep to waking up. Now when a human being has fallen asleep, his spirit-soul nature lives. The scientist of spirit can compare what he perceives in the spiritual world with what the unconscious spirit-soul nature experiences from the moment of going to sleep to waking. He experiences the spirit-soul nature unconsciously in the spiritual world, draws himself again into the physical body on waking, and then makes use of the physical body in order to establish a relationship to his environment.

Now it is not sufficient simply to describe what happens to the body between going to sleep and waking, and what sort of organic physical processes take place in it. For significant things also happen to the spirit-soul nature at the same time. The soul is quite different when it awakens and returns to the body from when it leaves the body. And in entering the body once more it can happen — as in ordinary life — that the spirit-soul nature simply submerges into the body and makes use of the body, and having penetrated it like a fast moving arrow it becomes active and uses the body as a means of perception. But it can also happen that the forces, the content that the spirit-soul nature has acquired from the moment of sleeping to awaking, are — if I may use the expression — for a moment too intense to enter into the body. What the soul upon waking has acquired since the moment of going to sleep, does not fit into the configuration of the picture that the body has of the soul, and so what then happens appears to be a reflection of what the soul has experienced unconsciously during sleep. Something like a mirror picture is reflected back upon waking, because upon waking the soul cannot at first be adapted to the body. In this way the soul clothes these quite different kinds of experiences of the spiritual world, which it has gone through during sleep, in pictures borrowed from our memory, from ordinary life, or which are transformed sense or bodily impressions. It is the eternal that dreams in the human being, just as it is the eternal in the human being that investigates the spirit, but it is clothed with the events of everyday life.

Thus we can say that in dreams the eternal in man perceives the temporal. It is the eternal in man that perceives what takes place in time. And in this respect dreams, despite the fact that the content of their pictures, which is taken from temporal life, is nothing special, even for the scientist of spirit, if it is a normal dream, are a real revelation of the unconscious eternal-spirit nature living in man, of the supersensible. The scientist of spirit is in the position to be able to distinguish between what dreams present in pictures, and what they are really based upon.

I have recently spoken about the various phenomena of human soul life from a different viewpoint in another city — a city where a great deal of work has been done on Psychoanalysis. Psychoanalysis deals among other things with the world of dreams. There were some gentlemen present who, as so often happens with the science of spirit, completely misunderstood what I said. In relation to what I said about dreams they thought they were very much more clever. They said: This person and his science of spirit, he speaks about dreams. We psychoanalysts know that dreams only have a symbolical meaning. We know that dreams should only be handled as a matter of symbolism, but he takes dreams to be something real! He is on quite the wrong path. — As I said, they thought they were very clever. But the matter in which they thought themselves clever, in fact, arose only out of their own lack of understanding. For the scientist of spirit does not take the content of dreams to be symbolical or anything else. The scientist of spirit who is accustomed to observing such things knows that what really happens in the soul during sleep can be the same with ten people, but when these ten people relate their dreams, all ten are different. The scientist of spirit knows that although the ten people have dreams, all with a different content, the same or at least very similar spiritual and unconscious experience is the basis for all of them. Moreover, the scientist of spirit would never simply take the content of the dream by itself, whether symbolically or not symbolically, for he knows that the same dream can be clothed in ten, a hundred or a thousand different ways, because the eternal regards the temporal in such a way as to clothe itself with it. The scientist of spirit therefore studies the course of the dream, the way in which tension is released, whether a rise or a fall follows. It is the inner drama, the type of rhythmical sequence, I would even say, the musical nature, that comes to expression in the most varied ways in the pictures of a dream. That is what he studies. Dreams are the witness of real spiritual experience; their content is a garment which clothes the experience. But when one is experienced in such things it is possible to see through the content to what can be experienced. This is the one aspect of the nature of dreams that the science of spirit points to.

The other aspect is the following. When the scientist of spirit progresses and comes to have experiences in the spiritual world, he notices that his dream life changes. Among the many who have already had practical experience with ways of the science of spirit are some who acquire a convincing idea of the science of spirit and feel that it means a lot to them by seeing how their dream life is transformed. They see that what normally happens in dreams is that there is a succession of quite arbitrary images, but then they see how it becomes increasingly full of meaning, and that finally they are able to direct the dream in certain respects. In short, the most varied people entering into the science of spirit notice that the changes which take place in dreams take dreams in the same direction as the first stages of real spiritual knowledge. In fact, it is by means of this transformation of the world of dreams that the scientist of spirit is able to get at the actual nature of dreams. He raises his dreams out of their temporality through what he has become as a scientist of spirit. Dreams then no longer have the tendency to clothe themselves with temporal things.

It is a great moment when the scientist of spirit has progressed sufficiently to dream not only the outer pictures that have symbolical value, but in his dreams to enter into the sphere which normally he would only enter arbitrarily. — It is a great moment when he learns how the spiritual world sends him experiences in his dreams that penetrate like an act of grace into his normal experience, and which really are no longer dreams, although in certain respects they may appear like dreams. Thus the science of spirit shows that dreams flow out of the eternal spirit-soul sphere, but that the human being who has not managed to be conscious of this eternal spirit-soul sphere clothes the events which happen between going to sleep and waking up with his memories, with his impressions of everyday life.

Whether dreams are subconscious or unconscious events, or whether they are grasped by the scientist of spirit, they can be regarded as something healthy and normal. This is more than can be said of the other border areas. It is remarkable that there are philosophers, Eduard von Hartmann among them, who compare dream pictures, the origin of which we have just recognized, with hallucinations and visions. Whereas dream pictures originate in the spirit-soul sphere, and only come into being in coming into contact with the bodily nature, visions and hallucinations are very much connected in their origin with the bodily nature. And whereas dreams in their essential experience flow out of the spirit-soul sphere and the bodily nature only provides the cause of their appearance, the bodily constitution is the cause of everything in the way of hallucinations, visions, somnambulism, mediumism and everything abnormal of this sort that enters human soul life. You can see a characteristic of human experience purely from the viewpoint of the science of spirit, to which the scientific viewpoint can easily be added, when you understand that it all depends upon looking at man as a being with body, soul and spirit, that he has a relationship of the spirit to the body only indirectly through the soul. The soul takes its place in the center. Even when dreaming, a human being cannot simply establish a relationship of his spirit to the body, but only indirectly with the help of the soul. In normal life the soul is an intermediary between the spirit and the body. What happens in the human organism when certain abnormal phenomena in spirit-soul life are produced, is that the normal relationship of the spirit to the body through the soul, where the spirit first works upon the soul and then the soul upon the body, is broken because of temporary or permanent illnesses in the organism, which then blot out the proper functioning of the soul. This elimination is not occasioned by the outer sense organs, but rather by the inner organs. If certain organs are diseased, then the spirit-soul nature cannot get hold of the whole body by means of which it establishes a relationship to the outer world, but it often has to make use of the body without the diseased organs. Then instead of using the soul, the spirit enters into a direct relationship with the body. In a sense, the soul is by-passed. This brings irregularities into the consciousness; the consciousness is broken through. If something spiritual is experienced without being mediated by the soul because a particular organ of the brain or the nervous system or the circulation is diseased, if a spiritual experience is not received so that the soul can use the body in the right way for the experience to be digested properly in the soul, then the spirit has an immediate effect upon the body, and does not work through the mediation of the soul. The immediate experience of the spirit — for it is an experience of the spirit, even if it is such that it penetrates the human constitution in an abnormal and unhealthy way — turns into hallucinations and visions. The science of spirit has nothing to do with this sort of thing.

The aim of the science of spirit is not to break down the relationship existing in normal life between body, soul and spirit, but to make the life of the soul richer, so that the relationship of the spirit to the body is brought about by a rich soul life. A poverty-stricken soul life can come about, however, when by illness a human being is prevented from using his whole body to establish a relationship with his environment. These kinds of experiences — visions and hallucinations — that do not have the same relationship to spiritual life that dreams have, must be regarded from the viewpoint of the science of spirit as being spiritual experiences, but not such as have more value than our ordinary sense perception; in fact, they have less value. For in this kind of irregular spiritual experience like hallucinations, visions, somnambulistic speech and action, mediumism, (which is an artificial kind of somnambulism) the human being is less connected with his environment than he is in his sense perception. This is the important thing. This is what must be realized.

In order not only to perceive his environment but also to arrive at a reasonable and logical understanding of it, a human being needs what one calls an ability to make judgments about the world, and for this he needs the use of the whole body. If the body is formed abnormally, he cannot form a sensible judgment about what is presented to him spiritually. Whereas the human being, when awake, can grasp with reason what he experiences in dreams, he is not in a position to transform what he experiences in hallucinations and visions into the normal experience of his waking condition, and to understand it.

Now the significant thing is that when the body, viewed outwardly, reveals such abnormalities, there are apparently spiritual experiences — this the scientist of spirit admits — only they should not be induced. If they appear naturally, they are the evidence of disease; if they are induced artificially, they lead to disease. Even good and important scientists go astray in these things which are, after all, phenomena of life itself, when they investigate them in an external way in the laboratory, and seek to explain them according to formulas of the scientific method. I would like to cite an instance, which I have mentioned before, because it is a typical example of how much scientists long to penetrate into what they call the supersensible sphere but at the same time do not want to approach the science of spirit, preferring to stick to their own normal scientific methods. I am not discussing this case because I wish to take a stand on its truth or untruth, but only to show how an irreproachable and outstanding scientist of the present time acts in relation to the sphere of the spirit and supersensible.

It is the case which Sir Oliver Lodge describes at considerable length in a long book, and which has aroused so much attention for such things do not often reach us from the front-line of battle. The events are as follows. The son of the famous scientist was at the battle-front in France. The father received a letter in London written from America, informing him that a medium has said that something important and decisive was about to happen to his son, but that the soul of a deceased friend of Oliver Lodge would take the son under his wing at this decisive moment. — Naturally this is a message that can be taken in various ways. All sorts of things could have happened and, outwardly at least, the message could have been true. The son could have been in danger of his life and have been saved and the writer could have said — Of course, Myers, the soul of the friend, stood by the son and so he was not killed. But now the son was killed. So the argument then was that the soul of the son had passed over and that his soul was helped on the other side by the friend who had already been there for many years. Whatever had happened it would have been possible to interpret it in the light of the message, because the latter was so vague. — Sir Oliver Lodge, however, is a person who describes the events from a conscientious and strictly scientific viewpoint, so that the case can be understood by anyone on the one hand working conscientiously according to scientific method, and on the other knowing what conclusions can be drawn. It is therefore quite possible to glean information from the book about what really happened.

Now after Sir Oliver Lodge had lost his son, various mediums were sent to him. — In the case of a famous person there are always ways and means of sending mediums and somnambulists to him. Sir Oliver Lodge only wanted to go into this conscientiously, observing the utmost care imaginable. He then describes how the mediums bring messages, either in speech or writing, which purport to originate from the son. There is a lot in this that makes no particular impression upon the reader, as is so often the case with spiritualists, but one thing did make a deep impression on Sir Oliver Lodge. Even the sceptical journalists in the widest circles were impressed. And this is the crucial experiment that Sir Oliver Lodge carried out. It is the following: The medium said: A message is now coming from the deceased son; Myers soul is also present. Both make themselves known. But the son indicates that there is a photograph which was taken at the battle-front in France, shortly before he was killed. He is in the photograph with a number of his friends. The picture was taken several times. In one picture the son rests his hand upon the shoulder of a friend, in another his position is different, and so on. Good! The pictures were described exactly. But they were not there. No one knew about them, no one could know about them, neither the medium nor anyone else. It appeared at first to be nothing but a fraud. But the important thing is that after, I believe, two weeks a letter arrived with the photographs, which had still been in France when the medium had spoken. The letter arrived two weeks later in London and it was possible to convince oneself that the pictures tallied exactly with the description. The photographs were there — a crucial experiment.

Of course this was sufficient to convince Sir Oliver Lodge's and many other people's scientific conscientiousness. One can understand it. But as a scientist of spirit one approaches the matter from quite different viewpoints. Just because Sir

Oliver Lodge has described it all so exactly, we can discover the true facts of the case. If we are only a little familiar with the relevant literature we can only be surprised that such a person as Sir Oliver Lodge does not compare such a case, which, however odd it may be, can always be convincing if obvious points are not always rejected, with the countless cases which are known with somnambulists as — if I may use the expression — an infection of the sense organs with judgments of the understanding.

Who has not heard of a case, if he is familiar with literature, of someone who has a vision having the impression — in three weeks' time when I am riding I shall fall from my horse. He sees the visionary picture exactly before him. He even tries to avoid it, but this only helps it on. Such things can be found frequently in literature. They are called up by disturbances due to disease, when the body is not fully under control, so that what remains unconscious in a normal organism rises up in a refined form into the consciousness enabling a person to have long-distance view into space or time of things that belong to human culture.

Now upon reading through Sir Oliver Lodge's book it is clear that what the somnambulistic medium saw was nothing other than such a long-distance view in time. The photographs arrived two weeks later. The medium foresaw the photographs just as the other person foresaw his falling off a horse. This has absolutely nothing to do with a revelation from the supersensible world, but is only a refined perception of what is already present in the sense world.

In such matters we must be sure of distinguishing where the spirit has an immediate effect on the body. This is not something that leads us into the supersensible. It is just because the science of spirit sets out to lead the human being into the true supersensible world that it has to stress the necessity of understanding the nature of abnormal cases, in which a refined life of the senses experiences something which is only a message from the ordinary physical world, only that it is experienced in an abnormal way. I could say much about what comes to light by means of this kind of intensification of the senses, and which is based upon something diseased in the human being. What characterizes this second sphere of the unconscious is a predominance of the animal functions over the soul functions. The spiritual, it is true, is involved, but what Sir Oliver Lodge wanted, — insight into the supersensible world, — could never come to pass in this way.

If we wish to form a bridge between someone who is here and someone in the supersensible world as a so-called dead person, we have to do it with the methods of the science of spirit. We have to develop our own souls to find the way and not do it by allowing a dead person to speak through a somnambulistic medium. It is just such things as these that must be observed. Because the science of spirit keeps its feet firmly on the ground — one can enter the spiritual world not only in a general but also in a concrete way — it has to reject everything that is gained without the development of the soul, that is gained by means of hallucinations, visions and a refined life of the senses, which does not lead beyond the sense world and which says nothing about the eternal. Although the spiritual reaches into the human body, nothing can be found out about the supersensible except by raising the spirit-soul nature of the human being into the supersensible world.

For the science of spirit, therefore, the visionary world, the somnambulistic world, the world of artificial somnambulism, the mediumistic world is a *subsensible* world, not a supersensible world.

The time is pressing, and I cannot go into this any further, for I must turn to another aspect which can be discussed briefly, and this is the way the supersensible world appears in human life when we consider real art and artistic enjoyment. The science of spirit can follow the soul of the real artist or the soul of a person receptive to real art. What the soul experiences and later fashions into poetry or other kinds of art is just as much experienced in the spiritual world as what always remains unconscious in sleep or at the most becomes conscious for our ordinary consciousness in the temporal pictures of our dreams. But the poet, or artist generally, is able to bring what he experiences unconsciously in its immediate form while in the spiritual world, into the physical sense world, though still unconsciously, and to clothe it in pictures.

It has been quite rightly pointed out that it is not in its content but in its cause, its origin, its source, that real and genuine art has its roots in what the artistic soul experiences in the supersensible. Therefore true art, and not naturalism, has been rightly regarded by humanity at all times as a message brought into the sense world from a supersensible world. The difference between the poet and the seer, the person who perceives the supersensible consciously, is only that the seer raises his consciousness into the supersensible world for the time he has experiences in the supersensible world, and transforms with complete presence of mind what he has experienced there into images and ideas, so that the whole process is conscious. With the poet, the artist, the process remains unconscious. — He certainly lives in the supersensible, but because it does not come into his consciousness he cannot compare it with the spiritual world. After he has experienced it, he brings it down and clothes it in pictures which then became messages of the supersensible. The whole process which is conscious in the seer is, in its origin, partly unconscious in the poet and artist. What reaches into the world as revelation of the unconscious is what graces human life with beauty, and we shall appreciate its real value when we are convinced that true art is a messenger from the world of the eternal, that true artistic enjoyment brings the human

57

being near to the supersensible world, even if unconsciously.

We experience our destiny semi-unconsciously. How do we normally understand our destiny, which accompanies our lives from birth to death? Most people — quite rightly as far as our ordinary consciousness is concerned — regard the individual acts of destiny as something that comes to them from outside; they just come. This may be quite right and is right from the normal viewpoint. But there is another way of looking at it.

Let us assume that as a forty year old person or younger, as one who has a tendency to reflect, we consider what we really are in our souls and compare this with our destiny. And then we ask what we would have been if we had had a different destiny, if different things had happened to us. We would then make a remarkable discovery. We would discover that if we speak of what we really bear in our inner nature, of what we really are, and not about an abstract self, that we are nothing more than the result of our destiny. — If destiny were only a series of things that happen to us, a series of chances or coincidences we should only be the sum total of these chances. What we have suffered, the things that have given us joy, what has come to us in life that we have assimilated and has become part of our ability, wisdom and habits in life, *this* is what we are — but it arises out of our destiny; we are this destiny ourselves.

The science of spirit also tries to study destiny, and tries to do it in such a way that its observation of it follows the same course as our normal conceptual life, without the human being doing anything about it. I say this to make clear the significant factor I wish to express. Imagine that you remember something that happened a long time ago, that you experienced when you were ten or seventeen. The memory has a particular characteristic. When the experience took place you were present with your whole mind, you did not only experience what you recall as an image, but you were wholly present. Consider how very different it is to remember how you felt and to remember the image of the experience. The feeling, the condition of soul, cannot be brought back. The memory-image can recall a kind of feeling, but pain that you experienced twenty years ago cannot be recalled. The image or idea can be recalled, but not the condition of soul, the pain. And it is just the same with joy.

In our normal memory of life our experiences are incorporated into the memory, but the feelings are not taken in and the image alone remains. We can therefore experience again later in images what we have experienced earlier. But now, what the human being does of his own volition in life in separating the feelings off from what is incorporated into the memory, can also be carried out in relation to the experiences of our destiny. In describing it, it appears easy, almost trivial. Should it be undertaken, then it belongs to the kind of preparation of the soul that I have been describing yesterday and today, and it consists in stripping of feelings all the things that come to us as acts of destiny. What is so characteristic of ordinary life is that we find some things in our destiny sympathetic, others not; that we willingly take to some things, but wish to reject others. Imagine that we would succeed in getting rid of this so that we could look at our own destinies as if they had not affected us, as if we were describing the destiny of someone else, or as if we could feel someone else's destiny as our own.

Let us get rid of it all for the moment — and only for this one moment, or we would become unfit to live properly — and consider our destiny! We have to look at destiny in such a way that everything connected with the feelings plays no part, as if we stood outside our destiny. Then, like a thought rising up, giving back to us in our individual personal lives an experience out of the past, our destiny, when looked at in the right way, stripped of its personal, subjective character, will of necessity and with the utmost conviction be seen as the expression of earlier experiences in life, which we have gone through and which are connected with the whole life of the human being and are the expression of the fact that we live through repeated lives on earth and lives which are spent between death and a new birth.

By means of this true view of destiny and of several other things, we can perceive how what we experience over the years as entering into our real and personal experience of our destiny, what is derived as a germinal force from earlier lives on earth and becomes a seed for future lives, — how all this has an effect upon our lives. What the science of spirit has to say about repeated lives on earth is not something made up by a fanatical mind, but is a result of conscientious observation of life itself, a different observation of life from what is usual, because it raises what enters semi-unconsciously into our lives and is revealed as our destiny — thus also a revelation of the unconscious, the unconscious raised into the consciousness.

Unfortunately I have only been able to describe to you a few aspects of the world which remains unconscious to our normal consciousness, and to show how the science of spirit approaches such things. I have only been able to give an outline. But it is just a consideration of the border areas that shows how the science of spirit is in a position to point out the region of the eternal, in showing how the spiritual is revealed in ordinary life in dreams in both a normal and abnormal way, and in showing just from its particular viewpoint how the unconscious is revealed in human experience. In studying the border areas in this way it becomes clear for the science of spirit that the human being is certainly able to reach into the sphere of the supersensible when he goes beyond the normal limits of his senses, that he can penetrate from the transitory to the intransitory, that he can establish a relationship to the eternal spiritual world through his own spiritual nature so that his spirit-soul nature, his eternal nature, can feel in harmony with the spirit of the whole world.

In describing such things as these one notices that the science of spirit can only be taken in the way I mentioned yesterday — that whereas it can appear in the world today because of the particular configuration of present day spiritual and cultural life, its content is true for all times — just as the Copernican outlook had to appear out of a particular configuration at a certain time. But there is, nevertheless, a difference between the nature of what appears in ordinary science and what appears in the science of spirit. Today for the first time the science of spirit is expressed in clear and well-defined concepts and ideas. But it has always been divined and desired in both universal and quite definite forms by those who have undertaken a serious study of the great mysteries of existence. One feels as a scientist of spirit, therefore, at one with those who throughout the history of humanity have been able and have wanted to give something to humanity.

Of all the great number of personalities who could be mentioned here, I will choose only one. I do not do this to prove what I have said, for I know quite well that in citing Goethe the objection can be rightly made that it is always possible to quote the opposite from his writings, to cite passages where the opposite view is proved. But this is not the point. A person like myself who has devoted more than thirty years not only to the content of Goethe's outlook, but also to the way in which Goethe approached the world, can only sum up what he wanted to say in such a discourse as today's in a few words which express a kind of intellectual joy in finding again what has only now been revealed by conscientious investigation in a tremendous presentiment of a human being, a presentiment which must have appeared before him when he wrote:

"If the healthy nature of the human being functions as a complete whole, if he feels his existence in the world as belonging to a great, beautiful, worthy and valuable whole, if this feeling of harmony gives him a pure and true joy, then the universe, if it could feel itself, would shout for joy because it would feel it had reached its goal, and it would be amazed at the culmination of its own evolution and being."

I believe that in expressing the harmonious accord between the inner being of man and the universe, Goethe wanted to say what the science of spirit sets out to formulate in clear, well-defined scientific terms — that man can experience in his inner being in various ways how his spirit-eternal nature exists in relation to the spirit-eternal nature of the outer world, and that the great harmony between the human individuality and the universe is actually present in the human soul. — For what makes the science of spirit into an absolute certainty? It is that the human being can take hold of his eternal nature by approaching the spirit of the world in all sincerity and truth as a spiritual being, the eternal spirit of the human being can take hold of the eternal spirit of the world.

The Science of the Spirit and Modern Questions

When speaking about such a subject as this evening's we must earnestly bear in mind that there are countless human souls at the present time whose experience of the various kinds of knowledge and of the tendencies of practical social life to be found today makes them long for a renewal of these things, for a new way of looking at the world. Such souls feel that in certain respects we cannot take for granted that we can continue to exist as beings with spirit-soul life and social life with the ideas, feelings and impulses of the will which we have taken over from the last century and with which we have been brought up.

Living in the civilized world we have experienced the immense progress of the scientific outlook on the one hand, and we have experienced the tremendous results of this scientific outlook in practical life and in technical achievements which meet us from morning till evening at every turn. But we have also received something else with these tremendous achievements of science and with the practical consequences of this scientific knowledge in social life. Whatever a person does today, whether in reading or whether in his ordinary everyday life or in whatever else he does, he constantly takes in from morning to evening scientific knowledge in one form or other. When he then faces the eternal questions of the human soul and of the human spirit, questions about the immortal being of the human soul, about the meaning of the whole world and about the meaning of human activity, he can only link them to what his own soul thinks and feels about these questions, to the impulses of his own actions and to what science has been saying for three or four centuries in a way in which it had not spoken to men of earlier ages. Earlier he would have received the answer through the various religious confessions, but even if he belongs to one of the latter today, the search for his answers will be influenced by his modern outlook. And in living this existence which has become so complicated and the whole style of which is dependent on modern technology, the modern person cannot help seeing how dependent on this technology is his life. And he has to say to himself: Fundamentally, human beings in the whole civilized world have become quite different from what they were when conditions were simpler. And he must then become aware and feel that today there are many questions to be answered about social life, about the way in which people live together.

We can even say the following: Scientific knowledge is such that we are compelled to recognize it, and the practical, technical results which our modern life has brought are such that we are compelled to live with them. But neither really gives us any answers to the great questions of human existence; on the contrary, they only produce new questions. For if we take an unprejudiced look at what science so significantly has to say about the human being, his organization, his form of life on the earth and so on, we do not acquire any answers about the eternal nature of the human being or about the meaning of the world and of existence; on the contrary, we acquire deeper and more meaningful questions. And we have to ask ourselves: where do we now find the answers to these questions which modern life has caused to become deeper and more urgent? For as far as knowledge is concerned, the achievements of natural science have not brought solutions for the great riddles of the world, but new questions, new riddles.

And what has practical life given us? Of course, all the means of our enormous and widespread industrial life and world transport and so on have been placed at the disposal of our practical social life. But it is precisely this practical life which presents us with ethical, moral and spiritual questions as to how human beings live with one another. And it is just this kind of question that concerns the minds of people today as a social problem and which often appears as a quite frightening problem to those who think earnestly and who take life very seriously. So we see that the practical side of life also presents the human being with riddles.

As against these questions which confront the human soul from two sides we can now place what the present speaker calls an anthroposophically orientated Science of the Spirit. This starts, first of all, from the foundation of knowledge and then seeks in the foundations of social life those sources of man's being which can lead at least to a partial solution of these questions, to a solution which is not only possible, but necessary, because it is quite clear to an inprejudiced observer that humanity will suffer a decline and be unable to rise out of the problems which face it concerning these questions of present-day civilization if life simply goes on as before, if human souls face such urgent questions and simply dry up, and if no new impulses for the renewal of social life are found out of the depths of the human soul.

What the anthroposophically orientated Science of the Spirit strives for is not directed against the knowledge of natural science. Anything directed against this knowledge, which has brought so much good to humanity, would be amateurish and superficial. But precisely because the anthroposophically orientated Science of the Spirit takes very seriously the fruits which natural science has given modern humanity, it comes to quite different results from those attained by the kind of scientific research which is practised in every sphere of ordinary life.

The anthroposophically orientated Science of the Spirit follows the same path, indeed, in one respect is continues further along it. I would like to make use of a comparison in order to illustrate and explain the relationship of the anthroposophical Science of the Spirit to natural science. In using it I certainly do not wish to link what anthroposophy has been able to achieve so far with an historical event of world importance and to put it on an equal footing with it. It is only intended to be a comparison — there are always people who wish to make fun of such things, and I will leave it to them to decide whether they wish to make fun of this comparison.

When Columbus undertook his journey across the ocean he was not at all sure where he would arrive. At that time there were two possible ways of looking at the problem of world travel (which, in fact, came into the world through Columbus) : either one did not bother about the great unknown which exists beyond the sea and stayed in the area of one's home, or one set out across the great ocean as Columbus and his followers did. But at that time nobody hoped to find America or anything like that. The intention was to find another way to India, so that one only really wanted to reach what was already known.

The scientist of the spirit who seriously studies the researches of natural science finds himself in a position similar to that of Columbus who wanted to reach something already known by a new route, but then on the way found something quite different, quite new. In following the work of natural science most of us do not get beyond the observation of sense phenomena and the ordering of them by the intellect. Or if we are equipped with instruments and tools which then help our observation, with the telescope, microscope, spectroscope, x-ray, and if we are armed with the conscientious and excellent method of thinking of modern science and then with all this set out across the sea of research, we shall only find on the other side something that is already known and which is similar to what we already have : atoms, molecules with complicated movements, the world, in fact, which lies behind our sense world. And although we describe it as a world of small movements, small particles and the like, it is fundamentally not very different from what we have here and can see with our eyes and touch with our hands. This then is what lies at the root of the world of the natural scientist. But if with the same seriousness we journey further across the sea of research, only this time using the anthroposophical Science of the Spirit, we arrive at something quite different. We do not meet the well-known atoms and molecules on the way. First of all, we become conscious of questions: What are you then actually doing when you investigate nature as has been done in recent centuries? What happens in you when you investigate? What happens to your soul while you are investigating in the observatory, in the clinic? And anyone who has linked some self observation with what he does will say to himself — your soul is working in an absolutely spiritual way, and when it tries to investigate the evolution of animals up to the human being and to penetrate the course of the stars, it is working in a way which was not followed by men of earlier times. But of course humanity has not always looked at these things in this way. People have not always said to themselves: When I investigate nature it is the spirit, the soul which is really working in me, and I must recognize this spirit, this soul. The results of an anthroposophically orientated Science of the Spirit are really reached on the path of scientific investigation. They are reached as something unknown in the same way that Columbus reached America. But what happens when we are engaged in true investigation is that we become aware of spirit, of soul, and this can then be developed further. And through this we then acquire a true knowledge of what spirit is in the human soul. And it is precisely the task of an anthroposophically orientated Science of the Spirit to evolve the methods by which we develop what is active in the soul of the modern scientist. But we have to choose a quite definite starting point for this Science of the Spirit and that is what one might call intellectual modesty. Indeed, we must have this intellectual modesty to such a degree that the comparison which I am now about to make is justified. We have to say to ourselves: supposing, for instance, we give a volume of Shakespeare to a five year old child — what will the child do with it? He will tear it to bits or play with it in some other way. If the child is ten or fifteen years old he will no longer tear the volume of Shakespeare to pieces, but will treat it according to what it is really for. Even as a five year old, a child has certain capacities in his soul which can be brought out and developed so that through the development of these capacities the child becomes different from what he was before. As adult human beings who have achieved our normal development in everyday life and in ordinary science we should be able to produce intellectual modesty and to say to ourselves: as far as the secrets of nature are concerned we are fundamentally in the same position as the five year old child with a volume of Shakespeare. There are certainly capacities in us which are hidden which we can draw out of our souls and which we can then develop and cultivate. And we must evolve our soul life so that we can approach the whole of nature anew in the same way that the child who has reached fifteen or twenty years approaches the volume of Shakespeare anew as compared with his treatment of it when he was five. And I have to speak to you about the methods by which such forces which are to be found in every human soul can be developed. For, in fact, by developing these methods we acquire quite a new insight into nature and into human existence. The modern seeking soul is in a way unconsciously aware of these methods, but this is about as far as it has gone.

There are, as you know, many people already among us who say to themselves: If we look back to ancient times or if, for example, we look across to the East where there are still remains, albeit decadent remains, of an ancient wisdom of humanity, we find that knowledge or what we might call science takes on a religious character, so that the human soul can experience a certain satisfaction in its research for answers about the world and its own existence. And because we see this and because in our civilized life anthropology has produced profound knowledge about such old ways of looking at life, many people long to go back to these earlier soul conditions. They want to bring ancient wisdom to life again and want to further in the West what is left of this ancient wisdom in the East according to the saying, *"ex oriente lux."* Those people who long for knowledge which does not belong to our age do not understand the purpose of human evolution. For each age brings particular tasks for humanity in all spheres of life. We cannot fill our souls today with the same treasure of wisdom with which our forefathers filled their souls hundreds or thousands of years ago. But we can orientate ourselves to how our forefathers did it and then in our own way we can seek a path to lead us into the supersensible. But the human soul has a fairly good idea that in the depths of its being it is not connected with physical nature, with which the body is connected, but with a supersensible nature which is connected with the eternal character of the soul and the eternal destiny and goal of this soul.

Now our forefathers of hundreds or thousands of years ago had a quite definite idea about the relationship of the human being to the world to which he belongs beyond birth and death. When they entered on the path which leads to supersensible knowledge, into the supersensible world, there arose quite definite images, and these filled the soul with deep feelings. And there is one image in particular which made people shudder who knew about it from the past. This is the image of the Guardian of the Threshold, of the threshold which has to be crossed when we progress from our ordinary way of thinking which guides us in daily life and in ordinary science to knowledge of the spirit and of the soul. Men felt in ancient times: there is an abyss between our ordinary knowledge and that which gives us information about the nature of the soul. And these people had a very real feeling that something stood at this threshold, a being that was not human, but spiritual, and that prevented the threshold from being crossed before they were sufficiently prepared. The leaders of the old schools of wisdom, which are also called mysteries, did not allow anyone to approach the threshold who had not first been properly prepared through a certain training of the will. We can show why this was so by means of a simple example.

We are very proud today that for centuries we have had quite a different way of looking at our planetary system and the stars from the outlook of the Middle Ages and from the one we think existed in the Ancient World. We are proud of the Copernican outlook, and from one point of view quite rightly so. We say: we have the heliocentric outlook as compared with the geocentric outlook of the Middle Ages and of the Ancient World, where it was imagined that the earth stands still and that the sun and the stars move round it. We know today that the earth circles around the sun at a tremendous speed, and from the observations which are made in this connection we can work out the framework of our total world picture concerning the sun and the planetary system. And we know that in a way this medieval world picture can be called childish when compared to the heliocentric system. But if we go back even further, for instance, to a few centuries before the birth of Christ, we find the heliocentric system taught by Aristarchus of Samos in ancient Greece. We are told about this by Plutarch. This world picture of Aristarchus of Samos is not basically different from what everyone learns today in the elementary school as the correct view. At that time Aristarchus of Samos had betrayed this in the widest circles, whereas it was normally taught only in the confined circles of the mysteries. It was only conveyed to those people who had first been prepared by the leaders of the schools of wisdom. It was said: In his normal consciousness man is not suited to receive such a world picture; therefore the threshold into the spiritual world had to be placed between him and this world picture. The Guardian of the Threshold had to protect him from learning about the heliocentric system and many other things without preparation. Today every educated person knows these things, but at that time they were withheld if there had not been sufficient preparation.

Why were these things withheld from people at that time? Now, our historical knowledge does not normally suffice to penetrate into the depths of the evolution of the human soul. The kind of history that is presented today offers no explanation of how the constitution of the human soul has changed during the course of hundreds and thousands of years. In the Greek and even in the Roman and early medieval periods human souls had quite a different constitution from today. People then had a consciousness and knowledge of the world which arose out of their instincts and out of quite indefinite, half dreamlike states of the soul. Today we can have no idea of what this knowledge of the world was. We can take up a work which at that time would have been called scientific. We can think what we like about it, we can call it superstitious, and as far as present day education is concerned, we would be right. But the peculiar character of these works was that people never looked at minerals, plants, animals, rivers and clouds or at the rising and setting of the stars in such a dry, matter of fact and spiritless way as is done today, because at the same time they always saw spirit in nature. They perceived spirit-soul nature in every stone, in every plant, in every animal, in the course of the clouds, in the whole of nature. The human being felt this spirit-soul nature in himself, and what he felt in himself he found spread out in the external world. He did not feel himself so cut off from the outer world as people do today. But instead of this, his self-consciousness was weaker. And one quite rightly had to say to oneself in past periods of human evolution: If the ordinary human being were to be told about the nature of the heliocentric system in the same way that it was told to the wise — if it were simply said, "the earth circles through space with tremendous speed," this ordinary person would suffer a kind of eclipse of his soul.

This is an historical truth. It is just as much an historical truth as what we learn in school about Alcibiades and the Peloponnesian and Persian wars. But a truth we do not normally learn is that the Greek soul was differently constituted from the modern soul. It was less awake in connection with the powers of inner self-consciousness, and the wise leaders of the mysteries were quite rightly afraid that if such souls acquired supersensible knowledge without preparation, knowledge which today is the common possession of all educated people, they would suffer a kind of spiritual eclipse. Therefore the souls of men had first to be strengthened through a training of the will so that they did not succumb when their self-consciousness was led into a quite different world from the one it was accustomed to. And the souls had to be made fearless in face of the unknown which they had to enter. Fearlessness of the unknown and a courageous realization of what was literally for such souls the losing of the ground under their feet (for if we no longer stand on an earth that stands still, we lose the ground from under our feet), a courageous disposition of the soul and fearlessness and several other qualities were what prepared the student of the schools of wisdom to cross the abyss into the spiritual, supersensible world.

And what did they learn then? This sounds surprising and paradoxical, for they learnt what we learn today in the elementary school and what is common to all educated people. This was in fact what the ancient peoples were afraid of and for which they had first to acquire the courage to face. The human soul has evolved during the course of the centuries so that today it has quite a different constitution, with the result that what could only be given to the ancient peoples after difficult preparation is now given to us in the elemen-

72

tary school. In fact, we are already on the other side of the threshold which the ancient peoples were only allowed to cross after long preparation. But we have also to deal with the consequences of this crossing of the threshold. We are at the point which they feared, and for which they had to acquire courage — but at the same time we have also lost something. And what this is that we have lost in our modern civilization is clear to us when we read what scientists who take our modern civilization seriously have to say about what we cannot know. Why this is so should really be explained by those who face such facts on the basis of a serious study of the Science of the Spirit. We have arrived at quite a different form of self-consciousness since the time of Galileo, Copernicus and Kepler. We have progressed to abstract thinking. We are developing our intellectuality to an extent which was unknown to the ancient peoples with their less awake kind of consciousness. And because of this we have a strong self-consciousness which enables us to enter into a world which the ancient peoples could enter only after being prepared. Even the most unbiassed scientists who speak about what we are unable to know and about the limits of knowledge show that we enter into this world through a self-consciousness which has been strongly developed through the thinking and through an intellectuality which people in the past did not possess. But at the same time we have lost the connection with the deeper basis of the world. We have become rather proud of ourselves in having achieved a heightened self-consciousness, but we have lost real knowledge of the world. It is no longer possible for us to achieve such connection instinctively, as it was in the tenth or twelfth centuries. We therefore have to talk about a new threshold into the spiritual world. By means of our heightened self-consciousness we have to develop something that will lead us into the supersensible world, which we can no longer enter instinctively as did the people of earlier

73

times. These people developed a heightening of their self-consciousness through self discipline in order to be able to hold out in a world which we enter without preparation. So now we have to prepare ourselves for something else. In order to do this we have to develop powers which are latent in our soul and of which we become aware through intellectual modesty.

Thus, rather than starting with something obscure in the human soul, we start with two of its well-known powers. In the Science of the Spirit we begin with two powers which are absolutely necessary in human life, and they are then developed further. In normal life they are only at the beginning of their development, and this development is continued through our own work. The first of these is the human faculty of memory. It is through this faculty of memory that we are really an ego. It gives us our ordinary self-consciousness. We look back to a particular year in our childhood, and the experiences which we then had appear in the picture of our memory. It is true that they are somewhat pale and faded, but they do appear. And we know from ordinary medical literature what it means when part of our life is extinguished, when we are not able to remember something in the sequence of our life. We are then ill in our souls, mentally ill. Such an illness belongs to the most serious disorders of our soul-spirit constitution. But this faculty of memory which is so necessary for ordinary life is, bound to the physical body, so far as this ordinary life is concerned. Everyone can feel this. Those who have a more materialistic outlook show how this dependence is manifested, how certain organs or parts of organs only need to be damaged and the memory will likewise be damaged, interrupted, destroyed. But this faculty of memory can also be the starting point from which a new and higher power of the soul can be developed, and this is done in the way I have described in my book, *How to Attain Knowledge of Higher Worlds* and in other writings. I have shown there how the faculty of memory can be developed into something higher through what I have called meditation and, in a technical sense, concentration on certain spheres of thought, of feeling and of the will.

What then is the peculiar characteristic of the images of the memory? Normally our images and our thoughts are formed in connection with the outer world, and they slip by, just as the outer world slips by. Our experience is made permanent by our memory. Out of the depths of our being we can recall what we experienced years before. Images become permanent in us through our memory. And this is what we use in meditation, in concentration, when we want to become scientists of the spirit. We form images which we can easily comprehend — or we allow ourselves to be advised by those who are competent in such matters — and these should be images which are not able to arise out of the unconscious, nor should they be reminiscences of life, but they should be images which we can comprehend as exactly as mathematical or geometrical ideas. The cultivation of these methods is certainly not easier than clinical research or than research in physics or chemistry or astronomy. It is, to be sure, an inner effort of the soul, and a very serious effort of the soul at that. It can take years, although with some people it can also take a shorter time; it simply depends on the inner destiny of the person, but it always take some time before this continual concentration on particular images can lead to any result. Naturally the rest of life must not be disturbed through these exercises, in fact we remain sensible and able people, for these exercises claim only a little time. But they have to be continued for a long period, and then they will become what one can call a higher form of the power of memory. We then become aware of something in our soul which lives in the same way as the thoughts which we have about our experiences. However we know that what

75

now lives in our soul does not refer to anything that we have experienced in life since birth, but in the same way that we normally have pictures of such experiences, we now have other pictures. In my writings I have called these Imaginations. We have pictures which are as vivid as are the pictures of our memory, but they are not linked to what we have experienced in ordinary life, and we become aware that these Imaginations are related to something which is outside us in the spiritual world. And we come to realize what it means to live outside the human body. With our faculty of memory we are bound to our body. With this developed faculty of memory we are no longer bound to the body, we enter into a state which is on the one hand quite similar to, but on the other hand quite different from the condition which the human being lives through from the time he goes to sleep until he wakes up. He is normally unconscious at this time, because he cannot see with his eyes or hear with his ears. This is the condition we are in when we use our developed faculty of memory. We do not perceive with our eyes and ears; we are not even able to feel the warmth of our surroundings. On the other hand we do not live unconsciously as in sleep, but we live in a world of images and perceptions. We now perceive a spiritual world. It is really as if we begin to go to sleep, but instead of passing over into the dullness of unconsciousness we pass into another world, which we then perceive through our developed faculty of memory. And the first thing that we perceive is what I would like to call a tableau of the memory, that is, a developed tableau of the memory of this life which reaches back to birth. This is the first supersensible perception.

The memories we normally have are of our life; we allow the pictures of our memory to arise out of the stream of life. This is not the case when we look back on life through this supersensibly developed faculty of memory. In this case in one moment the whole course of our life is drawn together into a single picture which we can comprehend as something spatial before us. When we achieve this independence from our body, the fragments of our memory which normally appear as single events in time now form a coherent whole. When we have become accustomed to forming images independently of the body — in the same way that a sleeping person would if he could — there is then developed what one can call a real view of what going to sleep, waking, and sleep itself are. We get to know how the spirit-soul part of man draws itself out — not spatially, but dynamically, though despite this, the first is the right expression — and how this normally remains unconscious, how the human being can however develop this consciousness outside the body, and how consciousness arises when the spirit-soul part again enters into the body. When this has been developed it is possible to advance gradually to further images.

When we are able to imagine what kind of living spirit-soul beings we are when we sleep, we are able, through working further on the developed faculty of memory which we have described, to recognize how the spirit-soul part lived in a purely spiritual world before it descended into the physical world through birth and conception. We can then distinguish the following: A person who is sleeping has a desire which is both physical and supersensible, to return to the physical body which is lying in bed and to revive it in a spirit-soul sense. We also meet this as a strong force in the soul that is waiting to be received by a physical body which comes from the father and mother in the line of physical heredity, but we also come to see how this soul descends from this spirit-soul world and penetrates the body. We acquire knowledge of how our soul lives in the spirit-soul world before birth; we come to know the eternal in the human soul. And we no longer merely rely on our faith concerning the eternal in the human soul, but on knowledge which has been acquired through supersensible perception. And through this we also acquire knowledge of the great going to sleep which the human being experiences when he passes through the gates of death. What happens to the human soul when it passes through the gates of death is similar to what happens in sleep when consciousness is not lost but merely subdued, only here it is the other way round: whereas the human being is strongly attached to the body when he goes to sleep and wishes to return to it, thereby retaining his consciousness in normal sleep in a subdued form, when he goes through the gates of death he acquires full consciousness because he no longer has any desire for the body. Only after he has lived for a long time in the spiritual world does he experience something which may be compared to the age of the physical body which has reached the 35th year of life. After having lived for a long time after death the soul experiences a desire to return to the body, and from this moment it moves toward a new life on earth. I have repeatedly described in detail these experiences of the human being between death and a new birth. When such things as these are described, people today often make fun of them and regard them as fantastic. But those who regard as fantastic what has been won in this way should also regard mathematical ideas as fantastic, for what I have described has been won through true and earnest scientific investigation.

And now we experience a tremendous and significant image. In a memory image we have before our souls something which we have experienced years before. We have what we once experienced as an image before our souls. But if what we have before us does not arise through our normal memory but through the developed faculty of memory, we then have the spiritual world before us in which we are when we sleep and in which we also exist before we descend to a life on earth. What we now experience is not what appears to the senses in the outer world, but what appears to the eye of the spirit, the eye of the soul. We have before us the spiritual roots of existence, the widths of the universe. We rise up and go past a new Guardian of the Threshold, we cross over a new threshold into the supersensible world, to what lies spiritually behind the natural existence to which we belong. The stones and clouds and everything that belongs to the kingdoms of nature arise like a mighty memory. We know what a stone or a cloud looks like to the eye. But now to the eye of the spirit something appears to which we are related because we lived in it before our birth or conception. This is the great world memory. Since this world memory of our own supersensible existence before our birth appears and since our eternal nature appears before the eye of the spirit from the world outside us, we acquire at the same time a world tableau of the spirit that is spread out in the world around us. We acquire real spiritual knowledge of the world. The Science of the Spirit must speak about such things, for it is something which must be taken into modern civilization just as the Copernican and Galilean outlook entered the world a few centuries ago. Today the Science of the Spirit is regarded as fantastic in exactly the same way as the new outlook of that time which was rejected as paradoxical and fantastic. But these things will be accepted into human souls, and we shall then also possess something for the external social and the entire existence of the human being, which I am now about to mention. But first I must point out that there is another faculty of knowledge which must be developed in order to acquire full knowledge of the spirit.

People will be prepared to admit that the faculty of memory can be developed into a power for acquiring knowledge. But perhaps the more strict scientists will not be able to accept the second faculty for acquiring knowledge which I have to describe. And yet, despite this, it is a real power for acquiring knowledge, though not as it appears in life, but when it is developed. This is the power of love.

In normal life, love is bound to the human instincts, to the life of desires, but it is possible to extricate love out of normal life in the same way as the faculty of memory. It is possible for love to be independent of the human body. The power of love can be developed, if by means of it we are able to obtain real objectivity. Whereas in normal life the original impetus for love comes from within the human being, it is also possible to develop this love through being immersed in outer objects so that we are able to forget ourselves and become one with the outer objects. If we perform an action in such a way that it does not arise out of our inner impulses which originate in our desires and instincts, but out of love for what is around us, then we have the kind of love which is at the same time the power of human freedom. That is why I already said in the book which I published in 1892 under the title, *The Philosophy of Spiritual Activity*, that in a higher sense the saying, "love makes one blind," is not true, but that on the contrary, "love makes one seeing." And those who find their way in the world through love, make themselves really free, for they make themselves independent of the inner instincts and desires which enslave them. They know how to live with the world of outer facts and events, and how their actions should be directed by the world. Then they can act as free human beings in the sense that they do what should be done and not what they would be led to do out of their instincts and desires. In my *Philosophy of Spiritual Activity* I wanted to provide a foundation for a new social feeling of freedom which would enable a new form of social life to arise out of the depths of the human being. And now I would like to underline this by saying that we must cultivate this love as a power for acquiring knowledge, for example in developing a sharper faculty of perceiving how we become a new person each day. For each day are we not fundamentally a different person? Life drives us on, and we are driven on by what other people experience in us, and by what we experience in them. When we think back to what we were ten years ago, we have to admit that we were quite different from today.

Fundamentally, we are different every day. We allow ourselves to be driven by ordinary life and what the scientist of the spirit has to do as a training of the will is to take this development of the will into his own hands and to note to himself: What has influenced you today? What has changed in your inner life today? What has changed your inner life during the last ten, twenty years? — On the one hand we have to do this, but on the other hand we also have to do something else: we ourselves have to direct quite definite impulses and motives so that we are not always changed from outside, but that we ourselves are able to be our own witnesses and observe our willing and our action. If we do this we shall be able to develop quite naturally the higher kind of love which is completely taken up into the objects around us.

We therefore develop these two faculties of the soul — on the one hand, the faculty of memory which is independent of the body, and on the other, the power of love which really enables us to unite ourselves with our true spiritual existence for the first time and leads us to a higher form of self-consciousness. With these two we then cross the threshold into a spiritual world. We then supplement our ordinary scientific knowledge, and through this anthroposophically orientated Science of the Spirit, every branch of science becomes more fruitful.

I can remember how the great medical authorities at a famous school of medicine spoke of a "medical nihilism." And they spoke of it because it had begun to be said that for many typical illnesses there were really no remedies. In modern scientific life the connection with nature has been lost, for we have no real picture of nature. This or the other substance is tried to see if it has any ability to heal a particular illness, but in fact there is no real knowledge of such things. Through the Science of the Spirit we can come to a real understanding of plant life, of each individual plant and of the great differences which exist between the roots, the leaves and the flowers, and we can come to understand how connections of a spiritual nature lie behind the life of the roots, the leaves, the flowers and in the life of the herbs. We learn how man stands in relation to this world of nature, out of which he has grown. We obtain an over-all view of the relationship of animals, plants and minerals to the human being, and it is through this that we acquire a rational therapy. In this way medicine can be made more fruitful. Last spring I gave a course for physicians and medical students, in which I showed how the art of finding remedies and pathology, the knowledge of various illnesses, can be made more fruitful through this spiritual knowledge.

And in this way all the sciences can be fructified by spiritual knowledge. In acquiring this knowledge, in uniting ourselves with what we are, with the spirit-soul life, which now works on our physical body, we come to a quite different kind of knowledge from the one advanced by ordinary science, for this latter only wants to work with logical, abstract and limited concepts about nature and human existence, and it is said: no science is real and true unless it arrives at such abstract laws. — But supposing nature does not work according to such abstract laws? We can talk about them for as long as we like, but we are limiting our knowledge if we are intent on a logical and abstract method, and if we wish to proceed with abstract experiments only. Then nature might well say: In these circumstances I will reveal no knowledge about the human being.

In approaching nature through the Science of the Spirit we get to know that it does not work out of such laws, but according to principles which can be reached only through an artistic way of perception, in real Imagination. We are not able to fathom the wonderful mystery of the human form, of the whole human organization by means of abstract laws or through the kind of observation which is practised in ordinary science. Instead, we must allow our elementary knowledge to be developed and to rise to imaginative perception. Then the riddle of true human nature will be solved. And so a view of the human being is given us out of the Science of the Spirit in an artistic way.

With this a bridge is formed, leading from spiritual knowledge to art. Knowledge does not merely assume an outward character for those who devote themselves to it in an anthroposophical sense. If they are artists they do not employ abstract symbols or learned theories, but they see forms in the life of the spirit and then imprint them into matter. In this way art is renewed at the same time. We can certainly experience it if we are unbiased and impartial. The artists of the past created great and impressive works. How did they create? First of all, they looked with their senses at the material of the physical world. Let us take Rembrandt or Raphael — they looked at this material and idealized it according to the age they lived in. They knew how to understand the spiritual in the outer world of physical reality, and how to express it. The essence of their art lay in the idealization of what was real in the world. Whoever takes an unbiased look at art and at how it has developed, knows that the age of this art has come to an end and that nothing new can be created in this way any longer. The Science of the Spirit leads toward spiritual perception. Spiritual forms are first perceived in their spirit-soul reality. And artists will now begin to create artistically through the realization of the spiritual with the same sense of reality which artists worked with earlier where the outward reality was idealized. Earlier the artist drew spirit out of matter; now he takes it into matter, but not in an allegorical or symbolical way. — The latter is believed by those who cannot imagine how absolutely real the new kind of art can be.

So we see how the Science of the Spirit really leads to true art. But it also leads to true religious life. It is remarkable how those who find fault with the Science of the Spirit today say: The Science of the Spirit sets out to bring down into daily life a divine world which should only be felt in exalted heights. Of course, but this is exactly what the Science of the Spirit wants to do. The intention is that the human being is so permeated with spirit-soul existence that the spirit can be borne into every aspect of practical existence and not just be something which is experienced in nebulous mysticism or exercised in an ascetism which has little connection with life. People believe they have already gone a long way if they have given others an education so that when their work is finished, and the factory gate has been closed behind them, they are then able to have all sorts of nice thoughts and ideas. But a person who has to leave the factory gate behind him in order to devote himself to the edification of his soul is in fact not yet able to experience his full human existence. No, if we wish to solve the great problems of civilization we have to advance so far as to take the spirit with us when we go through the factory gate into the factory; we have to be able to permeate with the spirit what we do in daily life. It is this outer, spiritless life which we have created, this purely mechanistic life that has made our life so desolate and that has brought about our catastrophic times. The Science of the Spirit fulfills the complete human being. It will be able to bear the spirit from out of the depths of the human being into the practical, into what appears to be the most prosaic spheres of life. When the Science of the Spirit, which can combine knowledge and religious fervor, enters life, it spiritualizes all aspects of our daily life, where we work for other people, where we work our machines and where we work for the good of the whole through our division of labor. When we work like this it will become a social force which will help men. Economic and ordinary practical life will be taken hold of by a science which does not possess only an abstract spirit in concepts and ideas, but a living spirit which can then fill the whole of life.

It is not possible to solve social problems simply by changing outer conditions. We live in an age in which social demands are made. But we also live in an age in which human beings are extremely unsocial. The kind of knowledge which I have described will also bring new social impulses to man, which will be able to solve the great riddles which life brings in quite a different way from the abstract kind of thinking, which appears in Marxism and similar outlooks, which can only destroy, because they arise out of abstraction, because they kill the spirit, because only the spirit can revitalize life.

This is in a way what the Science of the Spirit can promise of itself: that it can not only give satisfaction to the soul in its connection to the eternal, but that it can also give a new impetus to social life.

Because of this there has been no intention in the Science of the Spirit of getting no further than a mere mystical outlook. We have no abstract mysticism. What we have does not frighten us from crossing the threshold into the spiritual world and to lead other people into the supersensible world in a new way. But at the same time, we take what we have won in this way down into the physical sense world. This has resulted in the practical view of life which I have described in my book, *The Threefold Commonwealth,* and in other writings, and which are represented by the movement for the threefold order of the social organism.

There are some people who say: The Science of the Spirit leads away from the religion of the past; they say it is even anti-Christian. Anyone who looks into the Science of the Spirit more closely will find that, on the contrary, it is well suited to bring before people the Mystery of Golgotha and the real meaning of Christianity. For what has become of the Christ under the influence of the modern naturalistic outlook? What has become of Him as a supersensible Being, who entered into a human body, who gave the earth a new meaning? He has been made into the simple man from Nazareth, nothing more than a man, even if the outstanding man in the history of the world. — We need supersensible knowledge in order to understand Christianity in a way that will satisfy the needs of modern humanity. And it is precisely through the Science of the Spirit that we can attain an understanding of Christianity which can satisfy the modern person. Those who speak of the Science of the Spirit as being opposed to Christianity — even if these people are often the official advocates of Christianity — seem to me to be lacking in spirit, and not like people who have a right understanding of Christianity. Whenever I hear such faint-hearted advocates of Christianity I am always reminded of a Catholic theologian, a professor, who was a friend of mine who said in a speech about Galileo: Christianity can never be belittled through scientific knowledge; on the contrary, knowledge of the divine can only gain as our knowledge of the world grows and reveals the divine in ever increasing glory. One should therefore always think about Christianity in a large way and say: its foundation is such that nonspiritual and spiritual knowledge will pour into humanity — it will not belittle this Christianity, but will enhance it.

We therefore need a Christianity that takes hold of life, that is not content to say, "Lord, Lord," but lives out the power of the spiritual in outer activity. And it is just such a practical Christianity that is intended in the threefold division of the social organism.

The gentleman who introduced me at the beginning of the lecture said that I had already spoken in Holland in 1908 and 1913. At that time I had to speak about the anthroposophically orientated Science of the Spirit in a quite different way from today, for at that time what the Science of the

Spirit had to contribute as a solution to the questions of modern civilization was only to be found in the form of thoughts in one or two human souls. But since that time quite a lot has happened, despite the bitter war years which lie in between: Since 1913 when the foundation stone was laid, we have been working in Dornach near Basel on the School for the Science of the Spirit, the Goetheanum. This School for the Science of the Spirit is not supposed to serve an abstract Science of the Spirit alone, but is supposed to make all the sciences more fruitful through the Science of the Spirit. That is why we held the first course in the autumn of last year, although the Goetheanum is not yet finished and still needs a great deal to be done to it, and we shall also hold a second course at Easter, though this will be shorter. Thirty people spoke during the course in the autumn, some of whom were great experts in various sciences, in mathematics, astronomy, physiology, biology, in history, sociology and jurisprudence. But there were also people more connected with practical life, industrialists, people in business, and artists also spoke. As I have said, thirty people spoke, and they showed how the results of spiritual knowledge can be brought into the individual sciences. It was possible to see that this science has nothing superstitious about it, but that on the contrary it is quite rational in its inner, spiritual nature and thereby acquires the character of truth and reality. And it is in this way that we shall try to work in this Goetheanum.

The Goetheanum itself is built in a new artistic form, in a new style. If in the past one wanted to build a place for scientific work one discussed with a particular architect whether it was to be in the Greek, Gothic or Renaissance style. The Science of the Spirit was not able to do this, for it forms out of itself what it knows as reality, not only in ideas, not only in natural and spiritual laws, but in artistic expression. We would have committed a crime against our own spiritual life if we had employed a foreign style for this building, and not a style which arises artistically out of the Science of the Spirit. And so you see an attempt in Dornach to represent a new style, so that when you go into the building you will be able to say to yourself: each pillar, each arch, each painting expresses the same spirit. Whether I stand on the rostrum and speak about the content of the Science of the Spirit, whether I let the pillars, the capitals or something else speak for me, these are all different languages, but the same spirit which comes to expression in all of them.

This is in fact just the answer which an anthroposophically orientated Science of the Spirit can give to the great questions which humanity has about civilization. For the first of these questions about civilization is the one concerning a real knowledge of ourselves, suited to modern times. This is gained in crossing the threshold in the new way that I have described, in acquiring powers of knowledge which enable us to have a view of the eternal in human nature through the developed faculty of memory and the developed power of love. And through this we arrive at a new feeling, worthy of the human being, as to what man really is. In meeting our neighbors we notice in them what is born out of the spiritual world, and see in them a part of this spiritual world. The ethical aspect of human life is then ennobled, social life is ennobled by the spirit. That is the answer to the second question, the question about human social life.

And the third great question of present day civilization is this. The human being can know: In what I do in my actions on the earth I am not only the being that stands here and whose action only has a meaning between birth and death, but what I do on the earth has a meaning for the whole world — it becomes a part of the whole world. When I develop social ideas I am developing something that has meaning for the whole world.

SUPERSENSIBLE
IN MAN AND WORLD

Any unprejudiced person who shares in the life of the present with wakeful understanding and with a wakeful heart as well, is bound to feel that we are living in a time in which man is faced by severe hindrances. The times have become more difficult, but it would be a mistake to look for the causes of this only in the outer world. After all, what we meet in the outer world, so far as this is composed of human actions, has its roots in the depths of the human soul. It is not always noticed how man gradually loses his strength and confidence, his capability, and his comprehensive overview of his life, unless from the depths of his soul and spirit he can form a conception of life through which he can be inwardly renewed.

This is not always realized because it is not understood how even the physical powers of the human being, which we use in the external world, are fundamentally dependent upon the life of the soul, which with its movement permeates our whole human being. And so anyone who is concerned about a positive development of our present civilization upon a wide front - for it is not a matter of particular specialized areas - must occupy himself with the inner life of the human soul, and must ask how from its depths powers can awaken for work, for a comprehensive view of life, and for the ability to fulfil our life's general tasks in the way that is necessary.

If we contemplate that conflict which for many people is present today in an unconscious way, it meets us as the consequence, both for our heads and even more for our hearts, of those achievements in knowledge, won in recent centuries by the scientific view of the world.

This scientific view of the world has achieved triumph after triumph, and has transformed the whole of modern life. All that we meet in the external world today, particularly as city-dwellers, is indeed a result of contemporary scientific thought as it has developed in recent centuries.

But quite distinct from this scientific thought there is something which springs from the needs of the heart, indeed form the needs of the whole human being: the moral and religious conception of the world. If we look round a little in human history, we have to say that the further we go back the more we find that in earlier times man derived what he considered to be knowledge from a moral and religious conception of the world. When he looked out upon nature, he believed that behind the phenomena of nature everywhere he could perceive leading and guiding spiritual beings. When he looked inward upon his soul, upon his own being, he thought that this divine spiritual leadership and guidance went on here too, and he assumed that if he even moved his arm or walked in everyday life, this depended upon an activity of the divine, spiritual leaders.

A view of nature, as we have it today in so great a form, the man of the past did not possess. Many examples make this evident. Consider the close relationship which existed for human thought in earlier times between illness and death on the one hand, and what was called sin on the other. It was believed that man could only become sick for moral reasons. In particular it was believed in ancient times that the human race was subject to death because of a primeval sin. Everywhere one looked, one did not see natural phenomena in our present sense, but the power and the work of divine, spiritual beings whose field within the human race itself was the moral conception of the world, and to whom men's hearts turned when they wished to feel themselves in the spiritual, eternal kernel of their being, within the bosom of the cosmic Godhead.

No view of nature existed separate from this moral, religious conception of the world. Today, for his moral and religious conception of the world man really has only remnants of what has been handed down to him from ancient times, when this moral and religious picture of the world was the only thing, without a separate view of nature.

Today we see this wonderfully developed conception of nature, in which man is included; in particular the nineteenth century learned to think about man's formation from natural causes, evolving out of lower animal forms. The nineteenth century, and still more the beginning of the twentieth, has learned to think that all our bodily members and our capacities for life are, fundamentally speaking, the natural consequence of heredity. Recently man himself has been placed into the natural order. We see everywhere processes according to natural law, which we cannot relate directly to anything moral.

The way plants grow, how electricity and magnetism work in natural processes, how the evolution of the animals and indeed the physical evolution of man proceeds, - all this, which science has formulated with such clarity, takes a form into which moral ideas cannot be brought directly. And though man can have an intimate joy and pleasure, and even a certain aesthetic devotion toward nature, he cannot have a religious relationship to the cosmic order when he contemplates that picture of nature provided by science today.

So modern man has come to see true existence and reality only in nature. But in his heart the need for a moral order struggles toward expression; he has a deep need to be related to something beyond the range of the senses, distinct from all that is perceptible by the senses in nature; he has the impulse to have a religious feeling toward powers which cannot speak to him out of natural laws. Modern man comes more and more into confusion, through the attempt to preserve the old traditions for the sake of a moral and religious view of the world. He finds himself in an ever-increasing conflict with the modern view of nature. Thus present-day man is in a divided condition when he looks at a world which appears to him as composed from natural laws and, according to his hypothesis, moving toward an end which these laws determine.

In contrast with this, there is the other way of looking at the world, of which he says that it alone makes him truly man; in contrast with this, there are moral feeling and religious devotion. And man has to ask the great and anxious question: Can I give any reality to my moral perceptions when nature gives them no reality? Can I direct my religious feelings toward anything, honorably and truthfully, since it cannot be directed to natural laws alone?

Thus it appears to man as if his moral ideas and religious feelings were beginning to hang in the air as something abstract for his soul, as if when the earth comes to an end through the dispersal of warmth they too were condemned to be buried and lost in a cosmos that consists of nothing but natural law.

In this way the man of the present time is placed in profound conflict. He does not always realize this conflict consciously. But he is conscious of something else: that he does not know his way about in the world, that he lacks strength and joyfulness for his work in the world. Often in order to have something his moral and religious nature can take hold of, he turns back to all kinds of old conceptions of world, to mystical, or as is said, occult conceptions. These he revives because he cannot find any knowledge about the supersensible element in man and the world from his present-day surroundings.

Nevertheless this supersensible element in the world and in man can be found: how it can be found, we shall now consider.

Something has always been felt as standing between what is purely moral and religious on the one hand and the natural, visible order on the other - something which appears in man himself in the course of his development. This has been seen differently in ancient times, where everything was regarded in a moral and religious way. Nevertheless, even today it is one-sided to regard such human qualities simply as part of the natural order. There are three things in man which swing to and fro, so to speak, between what is felt as the super-sensible in the human being and what is simply natural. Perhaps it will appear strange to you that I emphasize these three phenomena of human nature particularly, but you will see that it is these which in their metamorphosis can lead us to a study of supersensible knowledge and world-conception.

The first thing we see in the human being when he acquires his first experience of life as a small child in the struggle with the surrounding world, is this: from a condition in which he does not yet have his own characteristic posture in the world, he achieves this characteristic posture for himself - the power of standing and walking upright.

The second thing into which man finds his way, is learning to speak. And only through speech - the unprejudiced observer of childhood recognizes this - is thinking developed. To orientate oneself in the world so as not to look down upon the earth with one's gaze like the animals, but to look freely out into cosmic space toward the stars; to be able to carry one's own inner being over to other men in language; and to bring the world into one's soul in the form of thoughts - an ancient view of the world regarded all this as bestowed upon man here in the world of sense from what is super-sensible. The connection between supersensible man and the supersensible world was felt when these three capacities of human nature were contemplated. That man is so built that from his form there grows the upright stature and the power to look out into cosmic space - an ancient conception of the world, concerned with the moral and religious world order, regarded this as a gift from those divine, spiritual powers which worked in man. And even more was the capacity of speech regarded as a gift of these powers. It was never otherwise in ancient periods of human evolution, than that man believed that when thoughts arose within him, angelic spiritual beings were living in these thoughts. Only in the Middle Ages did man begin to discuss whether his thoughts were only his own creation or whether divine, spiritual powers reveal their life within his bodily nature in his thoughts.

Thus these three gifts were regarded in ancient times as entering man from the supersensible world, and working and living within him as gifts from the supersensible. And so one referred to these three gifts which come to man during his childhood, when one wished to direct man, standing and living upon the earth, and having his work to do upon the earth, toward the powers of the moral and religious world order.

I will disregard at this moment those exercises which were undertaken by man in still more ancient times, for example through the control of breathing, in order to acquire knowledge of the supersensible in addition to knowledge of the outer world. I will consider conceptions and exercises practised long before the time of Christ, though not in the very earliest times, and which were particularly connected with these three human capacities I have described.

We see how in the East, where in earlier times a mighty striving toward the knowledge of the divine spiritual existed, man sought first to develop what lies within his power of orientation - the power which enables him as a child to grow into an upright being looking out into the wide spaces of the world. Consider the positions, the bodily postures, which the wise oriental teacher laid down for his pupil in order to enable him as a grown human being to use in a new way what made it possible for him to orientate his position and movement as a child. In this way the teacher gives the pupil the power to allow the divine spiritual to work into his body. For one said: When from crawling the child learns to walk upright, the divine spiritual is at work. When the pupil of eastern sages crossed his legs and sat upright on those crossed legs, he assumed another position. If he became fully conscious of this position, then the world of soul and spirit could work into him; when this world works into the child it causes him to walk upright.

And when instead of learning speech, as this is done in the world of the senses, man turns speech inward - then he turns this gift of God into a power that can see and feel in the spirit, so that in this way he is able to bring what is supersensible in himself into contact with the supersensible in the world.

Therefore in early times in the East, a certain discipline of breathing was connected with the recitative, intoning speech of certain sayings, which were called mantrams, which were not spoken outwardly, in order to communicate with other human beings, but were in a certain way turned inward: They vibrated through the human organism, turning inward what we otherwise turn outward in speech, so that the entire human organism shared in the power and might of these mantric words. What the child poured out as a gift bestowed on him from the supersensible in language, the pupil of the oriental sage poured into his own body. For him the words did not simply vibrate outwardly to reach an understanding with another person; with him the words vibrated down into the lungs and on into the blood. They vibrated in the blood with the impulse of the breath, upward into the brain. And just as one who listens to our present speech, feels the impulse of our soul and its mood from our words, the oriental sage felt through the word which vibrated through his body, through this supersensible experience of the mantric word, the supersensible in the cosmos.

And just as the child develops thought from speaking, the oriental sage developed as a third stage, feeling the supersensible through the mantric word, - a kind of thinking. But this was not a thinking which was only within him, for the cosmos worked into him. As our soul vibrates out to the other human being in ordinary speaking, so the cosmos vibrated in through the word which he experienced inwardly. And what then spoke to him now was not another human being, and were not human thoughts - but cosmic thoughts; it was the spirit, it was the supersensible of the cosmos, which poured into his own organism.

In this way men sought in ancient times to bring the supersensible in man into relation to the supersensible of the cosmos. Everything that has been handed down to us as a religious or as a moral view of the world depends upon a connection of this kind, which man once established between his own supersensible element and what is supersensible in the cosmos.

For a certain period man has parted from the divine spiritual element in the cosmos, within which he once experienced himself. Teachers who sought their way into the supersensible part of the world became rarer and rarer, and so did human beings who needed such teachings and wished to hear what such teachers had to say in order to gain from it nourishment for their souls. For a time man went through a period in which all that was to be developed within him, including his soul and spirit, had to stand in the closest relationship with his physical body. For as he was in ancient times, feeling himself entirely sustained within a moral order of the world that was not simply contained within him but permeated the universe - feeling himself sheltered within a divine world, which for him was completely sovereign over nature, - man could never have come to freedom. He could never have reached that freedom which becomes conscious of the ego as a firm support within man, and does not derive action from the intervention of a divine-spiritual working into and acting through man, but seeks the impulse to action within man himself.

Man had to come to this consciousness of the ego and to

this experience of freedom. This has come about, but now we stand at an important turning-point in the development of mankind. We have lost the old connection with the divine. It cannot be found by those who in all possible ways wish to revive the old paths in the direction of Gnosticism or oriental occultism, in order to be comforted for what they cannot find in present day scientific conceptions.

The science of the spirit described here is indeed often attacked as a revival of old Gnosticism or orientalism, but this is not the case. This view of the world holds that we can find the way into the supersensible through the same exact ways of thought which are used today in the knowledge of nature, if only we strengthen and develop these ways of thought rightly. It is true that what I have described as the three special qualities in human nature, which were regarded in ancient times as gifts of the moral divine world order, appear to the man of today, on whom the scientific conception of the world has a powerful influence and convincing authority, only as natural gifts of the sense world. As a matter of course, - and rightly from a certain point of view - the attempt is made to explain the peculiar organization of man's body as a result of the way man lives, regarded as a development from the life of animals. Thus the attempt is made to understand man's upright posture as a result of natural conditions. And language is studied in its relation to the natural organism and to the connection of the child's organism with the adult human being; and thinking itself is examined as something connected with the human organism.

How could it be otherwise? For scientific research has indeed shown that thoughts are very much dependent on man's natural organism. If this or that part of a man's brain is damaged, a certain part of the thinking activity may cease. Everywhere can be seen how through certain poisonous substances which work upon the body, the spiritual activity of man can be diminished. The habit of looking at everything in a scientific way has placed these three: man's orientation in the cosmos, his learning to speak, his learning to think, - within a natural, sensory world order, in a way that accords with it. Something else also has been placed into this world order.

What man becomes for the earth through his birth or conception can be believed to proceed from a merely natural order, for this can be seen externally. It is possible to look on the one hand toward birth, and to see in birth and heredity everything that impels and energises us as human beings. But if we look in the other direction, toward death, it is evident to unprejudiced consideration that nature does not take up into itself what we are as human beings, but extinguishes it as the flame of a candle is extinguished. To modern man it appears as if he himself were brought into being by nature, through the process of heredity at work in the cell. But it also should be evident to him that nature does not continue him at the end of his earthly life, that nature is not capable of preserving his human being, but only of destroying it. For the man of ancient times, when he possessed a moral and religious conception of the world, the great riddle was the riddle of birth; for man in later times, and for us still today, this has become the riddle of death. The riddle of the process of birth has become the riddle of immortality.

For when men could look toward the world of the divine spirit in the search for moral and religious knowledge, and could bring the supersensible in man into connection with the supersensible in the world, the question was: How did man come down from the worlds of spirit, in which he was living, onto this earth? The natural process in embryonic life and birth was regarded only as an external expression of this descent from the worlds of divine spirit into physical earthly life. Birth was the great riddle. - What has man to do here on earth? - That was the question. Today man looks in the other direction, toward death, when he asks the great riddle about the true nature of his innermost human core.

We can consider this problem from still another side. It is possible to believe that human moral impulses arise out of a certain perfecting of the natural instincts, which spring from blood and flesh, from the whole human organism, or from the nervous system. Certain religious feelings too can be derived from the presence of such moral impulses. Thus in a way the development of morality and of religious feelings can be derived from the natural sensory order. We need not speak of reward and retribution for moral and immoral actions, since this leads into an egotistical realm. But we can speak of the fact that if we accept the natural order as including all that is, what we achieve in a moral sense would necissarily be powerless in the world, and vanish away. Here the point arises: the smallest expression of magnetic or electrical power has its definite consequence within the universe. - That is the scientific conception. Then shall what is developed in us in a moral sense, have no consequence in the universe at all?

In this way too we look in the other direction. At a pinch we may regard the moral impulses as more highly developed instincts, but through a merely natural conception of the world the significance of moral impulses for the future cannot be understood.

A part of humanity stands before these questions quite consciously. He who stands consciously before these questions has then to turn toward what is here described as anthroposophical science of the spirit. But a great part of humanity stands unconsciously, more in the depths of feeling, before these questions. No longer can they entirely accept what has been handed down as old religious traditions, and yet they feel instinctively: This must originate out of ancient knowledge! Indeed, it did not spring from faith, which man is urged to have today; all religious creeds originate from ancient knowledge, from that kind of connection between the supersensible in man and the supersensible in the world, which I have described to you. But we cannot pursue this ancient path again. Since then mankind has taken on another form of development. This development could not have passed through this intermediate period in which man has achieved the feeling of the ego-consciousness and the experience of freedom. Indeed man could not have lived entirely in the physical human body, if the organism had not been utterly different during this intermediate period from what it was in those ancient times, where those men received confidence and recognition, who by means of positions of the body, by means of mantrams and the cosmic thoughts which were revealed to them, brought to human beings a revelation of how the human soul is connected with the supersensible in the world, of how man as a body is only transitory, but in his soul is eternal.

If a man of today attempts, as many in fact do, - unfortunately for real knowledge, - to connect the supersensible in his own nature with the supersensible in the cosmos in the same way as was done for example by the disciples of Buddha, through special positions of his body, or through the intoning of mantrams to bring about the revelation of cosmic thoughts within him, he will bring his physical body into disorder, since it is formed quite differently from that of man in ancient times; he will not be able to direct it to the supersensible. That human body of earlier times, which could be permeated by exercises in the way I have described, had not yet that firmness and inner consistency from which a strong earthly consciousness of the ego and a strong earthly experience of freedom are derived. The human organism has become more closely knit. If today a more exact physiology were recognized, as is provided by the anthroposophical science of the spirit, it would be known that in the human bodies of recent times the solid parts, in particular the parts containing salts, have been more strongly developed than they were in the bodies of men of old times, who could carry out exercises for higher knowledge in the way I have described. The man of today must therefore bring his own supersensible part into connection with the supersensible in the cosmos in another way. The man of today has to seek for what is moral and religious in the world order in a different way from that followed in earlier times.

The science of the spirit as I am describing it seeks therefore to enter the supersensible world from two sides: firstly from the side of thought, and secondly from the side of the will. It does this through thought when a man experiences his thoughts, which have done him such great service in modern science in the field of observation and experiment, no longer simply as a reflection of the outer world, but by learning to live with these thoughts in the silent interior of his soul. In this way a modern man can develop a spiritual scientific method, comparable to that developed by ancient man through his mantrams, except that the mantrams were closer to the sense world, and modern man has something more purely spiritual in the development of thought.

I have described in detail the long path which has to be pursued in this way in order to reach a real science of the spirit, which is a knowledge of the supersensible worlds. I have done this in my books, for example in "Knowledge of the Higher Worlds and its Attainment" and elsewhere. Here I would like only to indicate in principle how today one can become a researcher in the spirit in a way entirely suited to the present organism of man.

Not everyone need become capable of spiritual research, but some men can do this. Nevertheless, to a certain extent everyone can at least get as far as being able to test the results of this spiritual research if he is willing to do the the exercises described in the book I have named. But the one who seeks to become a researcher in the spirit today, should not do it through the more sensory method of intoning mantrams, but must do it through a purely supersensible exercise in thought.

We have attained to exact thinking today. If I look out into the starry spaces in our exact astronomy, an exact thinking has indeed been achieved in the physical and chemical fields; it is attempted even in the biological realm, in the examination of living beings. We are particularly satisfied today if we can investigate the external sensory world in the way we are accustomed to direct our thoughts in the solution of mathematical problems. Thus it has been said: There is only as much real science of nature as there is application of mathematics in it. For this reason we speak of exact science. Everything should be comprehended by means of observation and experiment precisely in the way problems are comprehended, which can be solved by mathematics.

Anthroposophical science of the spirit, as it is intended here, speaks of exact clairvoyance. Just as the scientist of today pursues his exact research, the anthroposophical spiritual investigator does something just as exact, but in another region. He gradually discovers that in the soul exist hidden forces which are not used in ordinary life and ordinary science. He gradually discovers that it is truly so, that in the quite small child the spiritual-supersensible and the physical-sensible are still working together without separation, but that the child then pours out into the external sense world what worked in him in a supersensible way, in his upright walk, in his speech, and in his thinking. All that flows down into the blood during the very first period of human life and vibrates entirely within the organs, is poured outward when man begins to find his orientation in the external world; it is poured out externally into speech, it is poured out externally, especially in thinking.

But we can take it back again. The pupil of the oriental sage sought to achieve the connection between the supersensible in man with the supersensible in the world mainly by the turning of speech back into himself; we in modern times must turn back thought itself. We have to say to ourselves entirely seriously: We have gone a long way in the observation of external nature. We have before us exact thoughts about the forms and movements of the stars. We have before us exact thoughts about the working of electricity, magnetism, warmth, sound and light. We look out into the world, and it is represented within us by exact thoughts. As researchers in the spirit we must be able to turn our attention away from all the thoughts which lead us out toward the stars, or toward the phenomena of electricity, magnetism and warmth. Just as the old sage turned his mantric speech inward and let the world Logos reveal itself within him, we must be able to direct the power of thought toward our inner being. Just as we live with the external world through our senses, which belong to our bodily organism and come to our aid so that we do not need to use our own soul's strength, we must find the energy to make thought so strong in our meditation that thoughts themselves, although they they are only developed within us, become as full of vitality as are otherwise the impressions of our senses. When you hear tones, see colors and feel sensations of warmth and cold passing through your body - consider how alive it all is, how intensively it works! And on the other hand, think how grey and abstract in comparison are the thoughts which you retain from the experience of the outer world! Meditation consists in that these thoughts which are connected with the outer world in such a grey and abstract way, arising within us through a passive acceptance of sense observations, are made so strong and intense within us that they become exactly like the effects of the senses. Thus a new kind of thinking is achieved. Meanwhile, the other thinking which is used in ordinary life and in ordinary science, is such that one feels oneself passive in its exercise. One feels that these thoughts are really powerless, are mere pictures representing the outer world. - On the other hand, that thinking which can be achieved by meditation causes us to live in the world of thought as truly as one lives in one's powers of growth, in hunger and thirst, or in the body's sense of physical well-being! That is the product of meditation. But one thing must be learned in order to bring the world of thought to life within us. One must learn to weave inwardly in the thoughts with our love.

If one seeks to become a spiritual researcher, this must be practised with the same devotion as when someone who aims at becoming a physicist has to practise for years in the laboratory, or one who seeks to become an astronomer has to work for years in the observatory. It is truly no easier to become a scientist of the spirit, than to become an astronomer or physicist. Everyone can test what the spiritual researcher says, as long as he takes into account to some extent what I have described in "Knowledge of the Higher Worlds and its Attainment."

Just as little as everybody needs to become an astronomer when he includes the results of astronomy in his conception of the world, so little does everyone need to become a spiritual researcher in order that spiritual research can become a part of our civilization and our cultural life. On the contrary: that relationship between man and man which can one day arise, and which must arise in a not too distant future if the decline of our civilization is not to become more and more rapid - that social relationship between man and man, which will become necessary and is really already necessary, will be positively furthered if that confidence finds a place in human social life, which recognizes that he who speaks out of the depths of his soul about the spiritual-supersensible worlds, because he has raised himself to them as spiritual researcher, deserves our confidence. Where souls are related in such an intimate way that the delicate realities of the supersensible world and of the supersensible being of man can be shared, those forces can work which alone can restore our social life on a firm basis. Hence it is entirely unfounded, and really springs from human egotism, when it is said: I shall not depend upon the knowledge of the supersensible derived from anthroposophical research, as long as I cannot see the things for myself. - Every man is so constructed that he is predisposed for truth and not for untruth. Not everyone can investigate the supersensible world, just as not everyone can paint a picture. But just as everyone can grasp a picture that an artist has painted, so can everyone, being predisposed for truth in his whole humanity, recognize the truth of the science of the spirit as it is intended here, not with blind faith, but through inner experience. This science of the spirit can itself be acquired only through a meditation and concentration within the life of thought which proceeds from ordinary abstract thinking to a pictorial thinking which is inwardly alive. In this thinking there live once more the cosmic thoughts. In this thinking man does not feel himself any longer enclosed within his body, but as standing upon the first step which leads to entry into the supersensible world.

Thus the man of earlier times took his start from something of a more sensory kind: the word which is directed inward. The man of modern times must start from something more spiritual, from thought itself which is turned inward, finding in this way his connection with the supersensible in the universe, and becoming once more able to speak about it. The words are no longer empty that can be found when in this way one has entered through an enlivened thinking into the supersensible that is within one's own being. Just as in the sense world we are surrounded with the many forms of plants and animals, and with all that shines down to us from the stars - so before spiritual contemplation achieved by pictorial thinking, the sense world fades and the spiritual world appears. One sees no longer only the sun in its physical splendor. One beholds a totality of spiritual beings, of which the physical sun is a reflection. Through this sun that appears physically one penetrates to the spiritual being of the sun. And in the same way through the moon that appears physically one penetrates to the spiritual beings of the moon. One learns to recognize how these spiritual moon beings lead the human soul from the worlds of soul and spirit through birth into earthly life, where it receives a body from mother and from father. One recognizes that in the spiritual being of the sun there exist those powers which lead man out again through death, and in this way can be known the course of the human soul through the supersensible worlds.

Knowledge is further deepened by developing the will, - not through bodily positions as did the ancient oriental, but in a way similar to the development of thought for exact clairvoyance, as I have described. It was a development of the will too, when one overcame the ordinary orientation of the body by crossing the legs and sitting upon them in order to obtain through this different position different streams of force flowing through man's being, so as to perceive the supersensible. Modern man cannot carry this out because his organism has changed. Modern man must work on the will directly. What the ancient oriental developed in a more physical way through positions of the body, - he also turned his body toward the east, toward the west, toward the south - for modern man would remain only a superficial affair. Modern man must take his will directly in hand. And again you will find in "Knowledge of the Higher Worlds and its Attainment" a number of exercises for the cultivation of the will. Here only a few examples will be given.

A man is accustomed to follow external events in the order in which they happen. Now he can transform his thinking, and imagine in the evening, for example, his most recent experience, and then what happened earlier, and then backward to the morning. In this way he pictures the natural order in a reversed sequence; he detaches his thinking which otherwise holds to the natural course, proceeding from the earlier to the later. Now he thinks in a direction opposite to the sequence of nature, and in this way he strengthens that will that lies within thinking. It is not now a matter of thinking itself, but of the will that lies within thinking. This is particularly so, if one attends to small details. For example, you can think: I went up a staircase today, and now I picture myself not on the lowest step, but upon the highest, and go backwards; I picture the whole course of going up as a coming down, and in this way detach myself from the real experience. In this way I strengthen the will which lies within thinking. I can give power to this will too, by taking my self-education in hand; I may say to myself: I have this or that habit and will alter it - in this respect in three years' time I will have a quite different way of life. Thus there are hundreds and thousands of exercises which are immediate exercises for the will, and aim at a transformation of the will so that it can make itself independent of the compulsions coming from the bodily nature.

In this way modern man passes through something comparable to the training of ancient man by means of the positions of his body. For we cannot go back to these old exercises, for the reasons that have been given. But in this way modern man succeeds in entering into an immediate relationship between his own supersensible nature and the supersensible in the world.

This can be illustrated through a comparison. How can the human eye be an organ of seeing? Now you can see from the phenomenon of cataract, which is a hardening of the lens or vitreous body, that the eye cannot serve vision any longer if the material part in the eye asserts itself. In certain parts the eye must be absolutely transparent if it is to serve for vision. It must be selfless in order to serve the human being. If we strengthen our will in the way that has been described, our whole body becomes a sense organ for soul and spirit, if I may speak paradoxically; then at certain moments of knowledge our body is no longer permeated by the instincts and desires of soul which makes our body opaque. It becomes as pure, insofar as wishes, instincts and desires are concerned, as is the transparent eye in its material constitution. And just as one sees the world of colors through transparent eye, so through the body that has become free of wishes and desires (it is not so always, but it can be directed in this way by someone who has practised the exercises given in the book that has been mentioned) one can come to the vision of the spiritual world - that supersensible world to which one belongs as super-sensible beings.

In this way we come to know what is truly supersensible in man. If one has once perceived how it is with man when he has made his body transparent in the way that has been described, when he lives in the pure supersensible world, - then one has solved in vision the riddle of death, for before one, one sees life without the body. One knows what life will be like when one has gone through the gate of death and has laid the body aside. One knows how life goes on in the cosmos without the body. In this way one's own human supersensible nature becomes known to one. And one's own supersensible nature, which as living soul goes through the gate of death, is recognized as something which is received into a supersensible world, just as it could depart from the supersensible world at conception. If through living thought achieved in meditation one thus comes to know the spiritual realm of the sun behind the physical sun, and the spiritual realm of the moon behind the physical moon - that is to say, those beings of soul and spirit who lead man into earthly being, and those who lead him out once more from the earth: - then one knows the supersensible in the world. And their one knows how after death our living soul is taken into itself by the living universal being , by the supersensible universe. Just as our body is taken into the world of the senses and summoned to death, so the human soul is summoned to life in the eternal by those beings who can be perceived in the supersensible part of the universe.

The course which human civilization has taken in this way, we then recognize as giving us the power through a culture of the will, - carried out in the present by means of exercises which are just as exact as the exercises in thought by which mathematical problems are solved, - to add to the natural world order a morality, a religion. We need this today. The course of human evolution is indicated in a magnificent way by the position in human history which a true science of the spirit gives to the Mystery of Golgotha.

How was it immediately after the Mystery of Golgotha had taken place on earth, - how was it with those men who were the first to give their faith to this Mystery of Golgotha? They contemplated the experience of Jesus of Nazareth, and they felt: In the man Jesus of Nazareth there lived the divine spiritual Christ-Being.

They felt that this divine spiritual Christ-Being had descended to them upon the earth, to bring them something that they very much needed. - What made it possible that these first Christians received the wisdom of the Mystery of Golgotha in this unconditional way? It came about through the fact that there still existed remnants of those ancient conceptions which were aware that man had descended from supersensible worlds into earthly existence through birth. When in the most ancient times man knew this quite clearly through his instinctive perception and through what was said to him by his intiates and his teachers, man felt that present in the spiritual worlds was a spiritual leader who had led him down into physical earthly existence. But men felt - because they knew how they had come down to the earth as spiritual beings, - that they too would go through the gate of death. And death was no riddle and no terror for humanity in the most ancient times, just as the animal (do not misunderstand the comparison; it is not meant to disparage the human being!) does not feel death as a riddle or as a terror.

That man learned to feel death as a riddle came only in the course of time. Death became a riddle only when man no longer understood the riddle of birth, when he no longer looked up into the worlds of soul and spirit from which he had descended, and thus he became inclined to regard all this as a mere natural process. Then death became a riddle for man, and the fear of death developed.

This was not healed by a theoretical knowledge, but was healed through the Mystery of Golgotha taking pla ce upon earth. And from the remnants of the old wisdom, human beings knew that the Christ Who had appeared on earth in the human being Jesus of Nazareth, was the same being who had led men as souls down from the worlds of soul and spirit to this earth. And the first Christians knew that Christ has descended to the earth to give men on earth what can free them from the riddle of death.

We see therefore what Paul himself describes: the connection between the riddle of death and what was fulfilled on Golgotha. We see that Paul describes to men that as human souls they can grasp in their thoughts what lies beyond death, only if they can look upon the Risen Christ, the conqueror of death.

Now it was from an old wisdom that the first Christians were able to understand, - although more in their feelings than in clear knowledge, - Christ as a Being Who had descended to the earth. That science of the spirit of more recent times, of which I have spoken, teaches men how to see into the supersensible worlds, leading man to a vision outside his body, when this body has become transparent in the way that has been described. Man then experiences himself in the world in which he will live after he has gone through the gate of death. This anthroposophical spiritual research must point not only to the human being Jesus of Nazareth, but to the divine spiritual Christ, Who descended from supersensible worlds, and can give strength to the supersensible in man. From this strength, developed in man by the Christ in accordance with Paul's saying, "Not I, but Christ in me," will earthly man receive the impulse to go as a living soul with the Christ through death. Then he will not enter blindly into those spiritual worlds into which he is received by the beings of the sun, but through the light which Christ brought to the earth, he is able to enter into this spiritual world AS ONE WHO SEES.

Thus such an anthroposophical science of the spirit can rekindle Christian religious life; in this way will the Christian religious life be deepened by anthroposophical spiritual science. Recent centuries have brought us the great achievements of the science of nature - in which however we can see no moral world order because nature reveals itself to us all the more faithfully, the less we project morality into it. Nor can we revere natural law as if it were itself divine. But if we apply the exact methods we have learned to use in mathematics and in the science of nature, to thinking itself, in order to raise it into imaginative form, and if we apply this exact method to our will, in order to achieve not an external and superficial, but a true spiritual magic - then we shall be able once more to connect morality and nature and religion.

What is the ultimate purpose of this Anthroposophy? It is to fill in the deep abyss which exists for modern man, for all who share in the world about them, even if it is unconscious: the abyss between the natural, amoral world on one side, the religious and moral order on the other. It will fill up this abyss, in order that in the future, within what is given to him through his body by the sensory world of nature, man may also have the supersensible in its power, into which there streams cosmic morality, not only human morality; into which there streams not only the order of nature, but the divine order.

Man will find his way into the future with those cosmic moral impulses which he can make into his own individual impulses, and permeated with the consciousness of God which has grown up for him through his spiritually developed vision. He will solve those significant questions and riddles which can already be divined if with full and unprejudiced awakeness one observes the world around us, aware of what can live in human hearts as impulses and hopes leading from the present into the future.

THE BIRTH OF THE LIGHT

When we see the rows of Christmas trees offered for sale in the streets, we might think that the custom of the Christmas tree is very old. However, the Christmas tree itself can show us how habits and customs change, for the Christmas tree which can be seen in nearly every home, is scarcely a century old. A hundred years ago or more one would not have seen a Christmas tree for sale in the streets, nor would one have found in the poetry and song of that time any reference to the Christmas tree. The custom of the Christmas tree is a quite recent one, and was adopted generally only in the latter half of the 19th century. It was about the year 1800 or so that the Christmas tree was taken as a Christmas symbol, though of course the Christmas Festival itself goes back to very ancient, pre-Christian times. Indeed, Christmas was observed in every epoch of which historical records are extant. In connection with Christianity, the Christmas Festival of the Christian Redeemer only from the 4th century, for in the first Christian centuries December 25 was not observed as the day on which the Founder of Christianity was born. Only from the 4th century was this date observed as the date of his birth. However, in the Roman Empire, for example, a festival was celebrated on December 25, and among the Celtic and Germanic peoples a winter festival was observed at about the same time. Even among the ancient Egyptians and among other peoples similar festivals were celebrated around the end of December, but they were concerned with a different idea than that of Christianity. It was only in the 4th century of our era that the ancient winter festival was related with the birth of Jesus Christ. the Founder of Christianity.

From this one might conclude that by doing this the Christian Church was acting in a way that from an historical point of view was against every tradition. But this is not true. Those who really grasp the significance of the Christmas Festival recognize the ancient wisdom contained it it. Such Festivals as Christmas, Easter, Whitsuntide are dates inscribed by our forefathers on the tablets of time, and to us, their descendents, is shown how our ancestors regarded the connection between man and universe, as well as the great secrets of existence. Those able to read the writing set forth by these great Festivals, those who can deciper the hieroglyphics which time itself presents, can look into deep, significant mysteries connected with the entire evolution of mankind.

I have already stated that the Christmas Festival was celebrated in every period history describes to us. Later we shall see what I really mean by this. - Now historical records go back as far as the third sub-race of the fifth root-race. (See Rudolf Steiner's Book, *Cosmic Memory, Prehistory of Earth and Man*. 2nd Edition, 1961, Rudolf Steiner Publications - Ed.) The period of our own sub-race, during which the science and civilization of the physical world arose, goes back to the 15th-16th century. This period was preceded by another sub-race which traces back to the 9th-8th century B. C., to the time when Homer sang his epics to the Greek people. This epoch has left us a record of the feelings and deeds of the fourth sub-race. Then we come to a still more ancient period, leading us back to ancient Babylon and Assyria, to the time of the Jews, to the age when the Egyptian priests preserved lofty wisdom which they set forth to the people at large only in an exoteric form. At this point the historical records cease. Our knowledge of ancient Persian history is gained from later records. The accounts of the wonderful religion of ancient India, the *Vedas* and Vedanta philosophy, are of much later date than are the thoughts of the Rishis of ancient India, who received their inspirations directly from divine-spiritual Beings and then gave them to mankind. From our present epoch, which will yet last for a long period, we thus can look back to the Graeco-Roman epoch when Christianity appeared, and into the age when the Egyptian priests were active. But if we go still further back, we lose the traces, for a knowledge of ancient Persia, for example, can be gained only by those who can study history along different paths, while still more ancient times are accessible only to spiritual vision.

Those wishing to understand the Christmas Festival must look back as far as that turning point in time when a new wisdom was taught to a newly arisen human race. This takes one back to the epoch in which the ancient Atlantean culture disappeared along with that vast continent which was destroyed by the Flood, to the time when a new civilization appeared, including the periods of culture just described. Of the Atlantean civilization no trace has remained, and still less have we external evidence of a still earlier culture, that of the ancient Lemurians, who perished through fire.

When mankind reaches a new turning point in its development, it must briefly recapitulate its past. In this sense, the three sub-races of the fifth root-race had to recapitulate three important stages of human evolution in brief sequence. In ancient India the wise Rishis looked back to a time when humanity experienced an entirely different stage of development, to a time when the two sexes were united in the single human being, so that no division between male and female existed in the human race. Thus the ancient Rishis looked back to a great unity in man; they looked back to the archetypal man, Adam, who was both man and women, and who in many spiritual teachings is named Adam Kadmon. This original unity in man was spiritually expressed by the highest cosmic Being, who was given the sacred name, Brahman. Originally

Brahman meant the divine unity, the single source from which manifoldness springs. However, this unity existed upon the earth itself only during the period when there was no division into male or female sex, when the world did not manifest its present diversity among beings. The divine, original unity of man - Adam Kadmon - reflects the divine Being of the ancient Rishis, and in this pre-human Adam Kadmon was peace, spirituality, clarity and harmony. He it is who speaks through the *Vedas*, in the words which flowed from the lips of the Indian Rishis. And this was the first epoch of civilization of mankind after the great Flood. At that time men did not speak of a Trinity, of a threefold divine Being, but only of an archetypal Oneness, of Brahman who included all and was the origin of all.

Then came an epoch when the Persian priests of Zarathustra, the wise Parsees, looked back to a period when the twofold human being - male and female - was born out of fire. This human being presented a dual, twofold aspect. Now man's birth out of fire brought into the world something which had not existed in it before· it brought evil into the world. In a human sense, evil did not exist upon the earth prior to the division of human beings into two sexes. This took place about the middle of the Lemurian time. Therefore good and evil exist only from that period, being present in the second half of the Lemurian age and the first of the epochs of Atlantis. It is of interest to trace the development of this twofold aspect of mankind in the spiritual accounts known as the Akashic record. You will find a description of the duality of man in my book, *Cosmic Memory*. This refers to the time when the human race was first divided into male and female, when the soul of man and man's power of will were at first allotted to the two different sexes. One who today deciphers the wonderful Akashic Records will be amazed at the way the two sexes appeared, for they were very different from what they are now. Following the wise direction of the leaders of humanity, woman first developed the soul element, and man the element of will. Thus a duality of soul and will exists. During the Atlantean time it appeared in the two sexes of the human race.

Through the fact that the soul entered into the human body, evil entered into mankind. And because mankind had to recapitulate that epoch which is characterized by the difference between good and evil, fire worship or the Parsee religion appeared, the twofold teachings of Ormuzd and Ahriman. In the religion of Zarathustra, good and evil were taught. No mention is made of a trinity, for this arose later in ancient Egypt during the period described in the earliest documents available to historical research. The prehistoric times recorded in the Akashic Cronicle include no knowledge of the trinity. Men experienced the need to look up to a third spiritual entity only when they were able to distinguish good from evil. This third element appears in the role of a mediator, and is most evident in the so-called Mithras Mysteries which originated in Persia and were spread over the entire world. In them we come to a trinity; there we find the mediator, the one who makes atonement, the redeemer who guides humanity from the evil to the good.

In those ancient times men always experienced earthly events as a counterpart of the divine. They saw in them a reflection of the activities taking place in the great vault of the heavens. If you study the Zodiac you will find there a sequence of constellations: Cancer, Gemini, Taurus, Aries. The sun, or the vernal point, constantly advances in accordance with certain laws, so that in ancient times the sun rose in spring in the sign of Cancer, later in the sign of Gemini, then in the sign of Taurus, and later still in the sign of Aries. At about the 8th century B. C. the sun had entered the sign of Aries, the Lamb. At the present time the sun is entering the sign of Pisces.

Events on earth follow events in the spiritual world. For example, take the sign of Cancer. Its true significance is not always grasped. Now we should understand the sign, for it points to the appearance of an entirely new age. The sign itself consists of two intertwining spirals. Whenever an important event occurs in the world, whenever one stage of development is replaced by another so that an entirely new infleunce enters the world, we have two such spiral movements that meet and interlock. One of these spirals indicates the end of the Atlantean epoch, and the other the beginning of the Arian culture. Thus our ancestors saw upon the face of the sky the sign for the dawn of the new Arian culture.

Then during a later period, the sun entered the sign of Gemini. Gemini, or the Twins, symbolizes good and evil, and it is this sign of the Zodiac that influenced the life of ancient Persia. Then the sun next entered the sign of Taurus, and this leads us to the third sub-race, to ancient Egypt. There we find the worship of the Bull, of the Egyptian Apis-Bull. In Babylonia we discover the cult of the Bull, and in ancient Persia the sacrifice of the Bull, or the Mithras cult. This cult of the Bull was brought down to earth from heaven where it was inscribed.

The fourth sub-race, the period in which Christianity appeared, begins with the entrance of the sun into Aries. This important turning point in history is indicated by a significant legend, the story of the Golden Fleece which was captured by Jason, the Greek hero. Another important turning point is indicated by the symbol of the Mystical Lamb hanging upon the Cross. It is the historical expression of the Mystery indicated by the fact that the sun, the regent of the world, has entered into that part of the heaven designated as Aries, the Lamb.

It is important that this whole course of evolution be understood correctly. The concept of the trinity appeared in human consciousness after the latter had comprehended the duality of good and evil. Various religions show this. Let us recall the Mithras Mysteries, which existed in many regions around the Mediterranean. Let us now enter one of these Mithras Temples. There a symbolic deed was performed for those who took part in the Lesser Mysteries. Those who participated in the Greater Mysteries could see these same events as real happenings in the astral world. Now I can describe for you only the Lesser Mysteries of the Mithras cult. The symbolical Bull appears, and upon his back rides the mediator, the divine being. The latter closes the Bull's nostrils, thrusting a sword into the latter's side at the same time. A serpent appears, along with a scorpion, while above the head of Mithras a bird is seen. Over the whole group soars a genius with inverted torch on one side, and on the other, a genius bearing an uplifted torch. They represent the sun as it passes across the vault of heaven. This is an image of human life as it appeared to human consciousness at that time. Man has attained the stage of development where he sought salvation within his own being; he longed for the third divine element which could guide him beyond evil, reconciling evil with good. Evil consists of the human passions which draw man down to the earth, down to that sphere represented by the Bull. The mediator who kills the lower nature by thrusting a sword into the animal's loins, is the representation of the immortal essence in man which can lead man upward toward his higher self.

Thus, during the time of the third sub-race appears a trinity, with a mediator between good and evil, and humanity learned to comprehend what in Theosophy is called Atmas, Budhi, Manas. The mystical mystery is fulfilled when the mediator appears. The idea of the trinity thus awakens in human consciousness. Therefore mankind was guided through knowledge of the unity, the duality, and the trinity to Atma, Budhi and Manas. Atma or Spirit-Man is the unity which will be achieved at the corresponding level of development. Budhi or Life-Spirit will be expressed in man when evil will have been overcome by good, when the duality in man will cleanse his lower instincts and desires on the one hand, and on the other hand will reconcile the higher, so-called fire-instincts or love, by consuming evil in the fire of love. Manas or Spirit-Self is the spiritual principle which already is beginning to rule in human evolution. As the Messiah or the Redeemer brought into the world a trend leading from discord to harmony, so the duality is overcome by the trinity, in which good conquers evil.

Thus the human race reached the point of perceiving its entire destiny in the trinity. But destiny within the trinity is seen to be an eternal, universal law governing man. We look up to the three-fold aspect of the Godhead, we recognize a divine Trinity in the world, and realize that we are dependent upon this divine Trinity. But first humanity had to experience in a real, direct manner that the divine Trinity had descended to the earth, embodied in a human being. This is the great event which marks the beginning of our era. The Trinity thus acquires a totally new significance in human consciousness.

We can comprehend the deeper meaning of the Christmas Festival only if we grasp the true significance of the Mediator. The duality developed out of the unity. Duality resulted in chaos, out of which harmony had to be created once again. This harmony could come about only through a Mediator. Harmony can express itself only in an archetypal, eternal law. At the time of the Mithras Mysteries this was expressed by the fact that in man himself people saw an image of the cosmic law which creates the everlasting harmonies of the universe. In the Mysteries of the Parsees, which I have already mentioned, we find a sevenfold initiation of those admitted to the sacred Mysteries.

Those who had gained some knowledge of the most elementary secrets belonged to the first degree of initiation, the degree of the "Ravens," for this was their symbolical name. The second degree was that of the "Occults," the third that of the "Fighters," for the sacred truth, the fourth that of the "Lions," and the fifth degree that of the "Persians." One in whom an awareness of man's highest spiritual nature had been awakened, that essence we call Manas, was called a "Persian" in the fullest sense. He was an initiate of the fifth degree, "Persian," and represented the destiny of his nation. If he advanced to the sixth degree of initiation, he no longer represented the individual nation, but the whole of humanity; he no longer represented the destiny of one nation, but that of all mankind in its development from the Lemurian time until the period of the fifth root-race. Such an initiate was called a "Runner of the Sun," a "Sun Hero." And all the Sun Heroes described in books are initiates of this sixth degree. Then comes the seventh degree, that of the "Father," and this was connected with the future development of mankind.

Now what does the name "Runner of the Sun" really mean? If we look back into the primeval periods of our solar system, we find that this solar system arose out of a chaos of heat. We find that the harmony of our universe was born out of disharmony; peace and order developed out of struggle and disorder. But how did those come about?

They came into being in the following way. The sun's course is so regular that it is impossible to imagine that it might turn aside from its path, even for a moment. The world is so firmly fixed in harmony that the sun's way through the universe is fixed and unswerving, and nothing can turn it from its course. In the path of the sun through the heavens the ancient Persian initiate of the sixth degree saw his own inner destiny. The sun within him, the spiritual sun, had to shine so steadfastly that nothing could make him swerve from the path of goodness and wisdom, even as the sun in the heavens cannot deviate from its course. One who attained the sixth degree of initiation was so convinced of this law that nothing could cause him to swerve from his path. Henceforward he was a "Runner of the Sun;" he was Sun Hero. And all the preceeding stages of his initiation simply pointed to this attainment of inner certainty, this inner sun quality.

Men who knew this Mystery perceived a profound harmony between man's destiny and the sun's course through the heavens. They said that the sun makes the days grow shorter and shorter as autumn approaches, so that nature dies and all its forces withdraw into the earth. When that time of year is reached which now is celebrated as the Christmas Festival, a turning-point appears: the light increases, the days grow longer and nature can reawaken. And ever since that time the Light was spoken of as a sign of revelation in the universe and in man, and human beings celebrated this Birth of the Light. In the East all men belonging to our root-race saw in the light the garment of the wisdom in the universe. In light they recognized the garment of the cosmic wisdom.

Today when we look out into the far spaces of the world we see light shining steadfastly and harmoniously from the stars. In reality the Spirits of Wisdom (In Greek, Kyriotetes in Christian esotericism, Dominious. - Ed.) manifest themselves through the light, which in the religions of antiquity was considered as the garment of cosmic wisdom. In ancient religions the trinity so manifested itself that first of all, the Trinity or primeval wisdom was revered, then was the duality consisting of light and darkness, and finally appeared the Trinity, including the illuminated human being, the teacher and mediator, Manas.

But a healing influence for mankind could arise only with the conscious birth of this cosmic harmony within the human heart itself. The light which exists outside in the universe, the light that is born there, must also come to life within the human heart in the present age. The appearance of Christianity is the external Mystical Fact which corresponds with the Birth of the Light. With Christ something appeared on earth which had existed from the very beginning, but had remained hidden throughout the epochs we have just been speaking of. During these cultural periods mankind passed through a slow repetition of three stages, but finally a new stage, a new climax was reached - the Light could be born anew.

Even as the light grows dimmer and dimmer during the advancing autumn and is born anew with the winter solstice, so the Savior, the Christ was born to mankind during the period of the fourth sub-race. He is the new Sun-Hero who was not only initiated in the depths of the Mystery Temple, but who appeared to the whole world so that even those who cannot see and yet believe, may be called blessed! (A reference to Christ's words in John 20:29, often quoted by Dr. Steiner. - Ed.) The natural result of this fact was that when people recognized the Divine Nature can descend right down into the personal element, the Festival celebrating the Birth of the Light could be replaced by the Festival celebrating the Birth of the Sun-Hero of the fourth post-Atlantean race.

This took place in the fourth century of our fourth sub-race. With this event something had entered the earth which before did not exist. This was the possibility that man could give birth to the light within his own being. He could do this becuase for the first time the Principle of Light had incarnated in a human being. Through this the Festival of the Winter Solstice was brought into connection with the Christ

Festival. The whole significance of the earlier sub-races is clarified by the replacement of the Winter Solstice Festival with the Birth-Festival of the Christ. Light and wisdom first appeared to man from outside. Now the light must be kindled from the innermost depths of the human heart, for Christ Himself must be born in man. This is why the Event of Palestine had to take place - a Mystical Fact and at the same time a historical Fact. (See Steiner's further explanations on this point in his book, *Christianity as Mystical Fact and the Mysteries of Antiquity*, Rudolf Steiner Publications, 1961.-Ed.)

Thus we have before us a historical fact, and this is the great secret which is so difficult to comprehend - the Event which occured in Palestine and really followed the course described in the Gospel of John, and at the same time was a Mystical Fact. But if you regard it in this way you will understand why from then onward the Godhead can be thought of as a Person, and that the Trinity, which before was comprehended differently, can now be understood in the form of Three Divine Persons.

Christ has become a Person, thus proving that the Divine Nature can assume a real form in man. A First-Born thus had appeared on the earth, and became the abode of the Divine Nature. From then onward this could become a permanent ideal, which can never be destroyed.

In the past, all the great teachers of wisdom, the Egyptian Hermes, the ancient Indian Rishis, the Chinese Confucius, the Persian Zarathustra, spoke the divine Word, for they were thegreat teachers. But with Jesus the Christ, the Divine Nature Itself first walked upon the earth in a living form. Before his time we had only the Path and the Truth. Now we have the Path, the Truth and the Life. This constitutes the great difference between the religions of the past and Christianity, for Christianity is the fulfillment of the religions of the past. In Christianity we do not have teachers of wisdom as they existed in every other religion, but a human personality who must at the same time be revered as a Divine Personality. This explains those significant words of the Disciples: "We have laid our hands in his wounds, we have heard his message," and so on. The emphasis is placed on actual ocular testimony, on direct sense perception; they not only heard his teachings, but experienced him personally. This gave rise to the conviction that in a quite unique manner the Christ was the Sun Hero of the world.

If we can comprehend this, we can also understand why the ancient winter solstice had a different meaning from that of the present Christmas Festival. In Egypt we have Horus, Isis and Osiris, the prototype of what appears in Christianity. In India we find Krishna, son of a holy virgin. Echoes of this myth are found everywhere. But the essential point, as we have already said, is that not only a trinity but a tetrad was revered. The divine Principle came down as far as the human personality. Before the Event in Palestine the divine Principle was enthroned in inaccessible heights. The teachers of wisdom of ancient times, the holy Rishis, reverenced this divine Principle as the unutterable Brahman. The pupils of Zarathustra saw it as the dual manifestation of Good and Evil. In Egypt we have the triad of Isis, Osiris and Horus.

But the secret of the fourth sub-race was the fact that the Divine Being dwelt among men, that it became a Personality. The most important event of our time is the fact that the Christmas Festival which always celebrated the birth of an initiate, now celebrates the birth of the greatest of all Sun Heroes, of Christ himself. Therefore in this manner we see these two things harmonizing in the universe.

If we consider the fourth sub-race and compare it with the time in which we ourselves are living, we see that the Divine Being has descended yet further. Today it has taken on a strange form, which must be understood if we wish to comprehend the Christmas Festival.

Let us go back to the time of the fourth sub-race, back to the 12th and 13th centuries. At that time the true nature of the Christ was fully comprehended by those who knew of this mystery. At that time there were comprehensive descriptions of the personality of Christ. For example, in the poem, *Heiland*, the conditions in Germany are connected with the person of the Christ. Christ stands firmly within the whole of mankind that the conditions existing in the various countries are connected with his Deed of Redemption. - So firmly does he stand as a personality within humanity as a whole!

But a different feeling may also arise. The belief in this archetypal image of mankind has been shaken in a certain way. Something has appeared which in some ways spells progress, since far greater numbers of people have entered the course of the further development of Christianity. But on the other hand, these people have ceased to comprehend that the very center of their thought, feeling and will is to be found in the individual person of the Christ. Fewer and fewer men dared admit that the essential point is the personality of Christ, and not his teaching. And at last this dissolved into reverence for an abstract ideal, into something spiritual toward which people strive. At the time of the first sub-race this Divine Nature was Brahman; during the second sub-race, it was Light and Darkness; in the third sub-race it was the Trinity. Then during the time of the fourth sub-race this Trinity had descended to the earth and become Person. The personal element descended yet further - even to the stage of the mere intellect which dissolved this personal essence of humanity, revering it as a mere abstract ideal.

In this time of our fifth sub-race a coming epoch is being

prepared, which must bring us to the belief in the new initiates, the Fathers. The initiates of the seventh degree are called the Fathers, as we have said, and in the world conception of the Science of Spirit we speak of the knowledge of the Masters, for in future there will not be only one Master, but many Masters, whom we shall revere thankfully and devotedly as the great leaders of humanity. The fifth subrace thus connects us with the future. The fourth sub-race appears to us in the very midst of the great process through which we are now passing, the Process of Advent, that is, of the three earlier races, symbolized by the three weeks of Advent, for mankind must briefly pass through once again the way the Birth of the Light was experienced at Christmas.

This Birth of the Light is followed by Life in the Light. And because of this, Christians cannot regard the Christmas Festival as something passing, for Christmas does not merely recall something past, for the Christmas Antiphon does not say, "Christ has been born to us," but - "TODAY Christ is born." (A reference to the Christmas Antiphon in the "Breviarium Romanorum," - *Christus natus est; hodie Salvator apparuit*, etc. See Steiner's reference to this in *Christianity as Mystical Fact*, 1961 edition, p. 139.-Ed.) The Holy Scriptures always speak of the present. This is important and significant. They speak of "Today" in the meaning of the Christ when he said, "I am with you to the end of all times."

This confronts us each year anew, revealing the connection between man and heaven. It shows us that in man also, something must occur which occurred in heaven. Just as the sun cannot swerve a fraction from its course without causing chaos, so man also must stay upon his course. He must gain that inner harmony, that inner rhythm expressed in the life of Christ, who was incarnated in Jesus....

This is the connection between heaven and man. Not only

does the sun follow its unchanging course, gaining new strength as the Winter Solstice, but in man it also brings about the Birth of the Light out of man's innermost depths, a new Birth of the Light, a Sun Heroism pertaining to the fifth root-race. This is why the Christmas Annunciation "GLORIA IN EXCELSIS DEO ET IN TERRA PAX" - "PEACE TO MEN ON EARTH WHO ARE OF GOOD WILL."

Inner peace will lead the evolution of mankind upon a rhythmical course, just as the sun has acquired a regular rhythm. In the sun we see an image for the eternal circular course of the cosmos. The sun has overcome its own chaos and has attained peace. In this sense, Christmas is a Festival of Peace, streaming out peace and harmony. If the Christmas Festival sends out the forces of peace and harmony, it will be celebrated in the right way. With the Christmas Bells we also hear the echoes of the whole striving of mankind, that has toiled and is toiling for a future development of culture, ever since the earth and its spiritual essence arose out of the great cold.

The future hope of the past ages of humanity came to birth during the time of the fourth sub-race. And the three epochs following that time must include a striving after what resounds with the Christmas Bells and Christmas Hymns. For if we understand the real meaning of the Christmas Festival we truly hear the harmonies of the heavens.